A Western Horseman

# FIRST HORSE

*The Complete Guide for the First-Time Horse Owner*

## By Fran Devereux Smith

# FIRST HORSE

*Published by*
**Western Horseman Inc.**
3850 North Nevada Ave.
Box 7980
Colorado Springs, CO 80933-7980

*Design, Typography, and Production*
**Western Horseman**
Colorado Springs, Colorado

*Cover Photograph:* *The Stewart family with the children's first horse—Beamer, a 7-year-old Paint gelding. Caitlyn Stewart is riding Beamer, and looking on are her parents, Charlie and Donna, and younger brother, Evan.*
**Randy Witte**

*Printing*
**Publisher's Press**
Salt Lake City, Utah

*Third Printing: February 1998*

ISBN 0-911647-35-X

# DEDICATION

To my dad, who can find something to appreciate about any
horse, and my mom, who always finds something to
appreciate in any book.

# ACKNOWLEDGEMENTS

In addition to my dad, a few other people from the mid-south
have strongly influenced my attitude toward horses and
horsemanship. I wish I had listened more closely to them when
I was younger. Max Payne can talk less and teach more about
using a horse than anyone I've ever known. George Midgett
never loses his focus on reining horses or how to have fun
while he's riding them. And George Tackett can always open
the door to a new aspect of the equine industry. My hat's off to
these men, and to all the men and women who share their
knowledge of horsemanship with someone else.

To my co-workers at *Western Horseman*, my thanks. This is
a great place to work because you make it so.

*Fran Devereux Smith*

FRAN DEVEREUX SMITH

# INTRODUCTION

THE FIRST *Western Horseman* book, *Beginning Western Horsemanship,* was written and published by Dick Spencer in 1959. Back then, many city dwellers weren't too far removed from rural backgrounds and, from necessity more often than not, had ridden horseback or handled livestock. There were few books on the market for western riders, but most people knew a little something about horses, even though recreational riding might not have been a high priority at the time.

More than 35 years later, however, another generation, one raised primarily on city streets, is learning to ride for recreation and sport. Practicing good horsemanship is important to these equine industry newcomers, just as it is to the many urban youngsters who fill 4-H horse clubs nationwide. Unfortunately, grandpa's no longer down on the farm to teach this generation about horses, so these future horsemen look to outfits like ours for information.

*First Horse* is the result of their interest and is suitable for both adult and youth riders. A child's potential grasp of horsemanship should never be underestimated since he or she often relates well to a mount—once the "why" or "how" of things has been explained. Youngsters seem more willing to communicate with a horse on his terms, in a way he can understand. As a result, children sometimes master the basics of good horsemanship more quickly than some adults.

*First Horse* was written with two purposes in mind: 1/ to help make the transition to horse ownership a positive experience for the first-time purchaser, and 2/ to help the novice rider learn the basics of good horsemanship and animal husbandry that can carry him or her through a lifetime of horse ownership.

There is a certain amount of risk involved in riding horses, just as there is in any sport. No one can determine exactly how any given horse or horseman will respond in any given situation, but there are guidelines that apply to most horses and most riders. The guidelines are not a guarantee for success, nor do they necessarily work for all people and all horses in all situations. But using such guidelines can increase your chance for a successful experience as a first-time horse owner and rider.

That's what is offered in *First Horse*— guidelines to keep you on the road to good horsemanship.

Many sources offer additional information about horses, but one is readily available to everyone—the local county extension agent. His number is under county government listings in the telephone book. Extension offices, affiliated with the U.S. Department of Agriculture and state land-grant universities, also provide educational materials and support 4-H clubs, including horse projects, around the country.

The 4-H horse program is a good one, providing a sound foundation for young horsemen. If you are a novice adult rider,

# INTRODUCTION

volunteer as an adult leader with a 4-H horse project in your area; you'll learn more about horses when you do. Many of the photographs in *First Horse* feature Colorado 4-H members, often demonstrating their horsemanship ability in order to pass from one level of study in the horse program to another. Thanks to them, shooting the necessary photographs for this book was an easier job.

Part one of *First Horse* addresses several questions that arise hot on the heels of your decision to buy a horse. Who can help you find a horse? Where will you keep him? How do you test-ride a prospect? What do you want in a horse, and what price are you willing to pay?

The book's second section discusses physically handling your horse, both when you're afoot and when you're mounted. Once you have the right gear and an idea of how your horse's mind works, you're better prepared for successfully haltering, grooming, and saddling your horse, as well as riding him. Your body position, the way you hold the reins, the cues you give with your voice, your hands, and your legs—all contribute to how effectively you communicate your desires to your horse.

Ask any professional horseman what he does when he has a problem, and most will tell you, "I go back to basics." Mastering the basics of good horsemanship not only sharpens a horse's response to your commands, but also gives you some tools to use for repairs, should a minor problem arise. Should a major problem arise, or should you just feel more confident about riding under an expert instructor, some thoughts are offered about taking lessons and hiring trainers.

Part three is about commitment—the everyday horsekeeping that comes with horse ownership. Even though you may simply want to see a horse in the pasture out your kitchen window, rather than ride him daily, the purchase of any horse entails a certain amount of maintenance and work. A horse requires feeding, exercise, deworming, health care, and hoof care on a regular basis.

Perhaps you are considering purchasing your first horse in the not-so-distant future, or possibly you already own your first horse. Maybe you rode as a child and only now, as an adult, have the opportunity to consider horse ownership. Whatever the reason, horseback riding appeals to you, and you have decided to pursue the sport.

No matter what your previous experience, with your first horse you share a kinship with horse owners worldwide. Although they may practice a different riding discipline or compete in a different event, each of these horsemen faced the challenge of horse ownership for the first time. They felt much the same anticipation and trepidation you may be currently experiencing, but now they are spending many pleasurable hours horseback.

—*Fran D. Smith*

# CONTENTS

# WHAT YOU WANT IN YOUR HORSE

## 1

*The Superstition Mountains of Arizona are a great place to enjoy trail riding.*

WHEN YOU set out to purchase your first horse, a first step is deciding what you would like in your ideal horse. What do you want him to look like? And more important, what traits should he have that will make him the most suitable horse for you to handle and ride at your level of horsemanship? For example, is pleasure riding your only desire, or is competitive riding a priority?

Either way, knowing what you want in a horse helps shorten the search for the right mount, and it increases your chances for finding a suitable mount. Realize, too, that although you are envisioning the ideal horse, there is no perfect horse. At some point in your search, you probably will have to make a trade-off, accepting a horse whose color, perhaps, is not your first choice, but who is more suitable in his training or disposition.

### Age

Age is a major consideration in purchasing a horse, not only the horse's age, but the rider's as well. A rule of thumb is that the younger the rider, the older the first horse should be. The idea of a youngster and a young horse growing up together is appealing to many people, but in reality that particular combination is seldom a satisfactory one. Either the horse or the rider needs to be knowledgeable in order to help the other member of the team learn about horsemanship.

A foal is a young horse who can be either a colt (young male) or a filly (young female). A yearling is a colt or filly at least

**Ask several horsemen to define a broke horse, and you will get several definitions.**

1 year of age, but not yet 2. As 2-year-olds, many young horses are prepared for future riding by being handled from the ground. They become familiar with working on a longe line, for example, or are driven from the ground. Some horses this age are ridden, generally for short periods of time, with the handler ever mindful of the youngster's immature body and mind.

During a horse's third and fourth year, generally, riding and training begin in earnest. This is a time of continuing physical growth and mental development for the animal. On the one hand, the young horse is childlike in some respects and hasn't completely figured out what is expected of him. On the other hand, the trainer is trying to show the horse what is acceptable behavior, encouraging him to become consistent in his responses, steady and reliable. For an inexperienced rider, the chances of accomplishing this with a young horse are slim.

A horse 5 years or older is considered mature. If a horse stays sound and is properly cared for, he can be serviceable until his late teens or even into his 20s.

Again, there are exceptions, and there are nice young horses to be found, but consider the odds. Your chances of finding the right first horse are greater when selecting from the mature horses available.

# Training

Although there are exceptions to every rule, the following is likely the most important guideline that can be given to anyone purchasing their first horse: Look for a mature, broke horse.

Ask several horsemen to define a *broke horse*, and you will get several definitions. Generally speaking, however, these are some of the traits of a broke horse.

1/ He is safe to ride and is easy to control.

*The Quarter Horse is often used for ranch work.*

2/ He responds willingly to a rider's cues to start, stop, and turn.

3/ He goes wherever his rider may ask him to go; for example, across streams, up and down steep banks or trails, or through brush.

4/ He is not apt to shy at ordinary things encountered while riding outside of an arena—a vehicle on the road, bicycles, motorbikes, wheelbarrows, strange-looking rocks, paper blowing in the wind, a barking dog, etc.

A first-time buyer should understand that there are many horses available for sale who have had lots of training, but are not truly broke, according to the above definition. Often this is because a horse has been bred, raised, and trained specifically for the show ring, for an event like reining, cutting, western pleasure, or roping.

But a novice buyer often purchases such a horse, thinking he or she is getting a terrific horse because he's been "in training" for 2 years or even longer. When the owner gets the horse home, he is unpleasantly surprised to discover he can't control the horse outside the arena, or the horse shies at everything imaginable.

A novice buyer who wants to compete in the show ring can also get into trouble by purchasing a horse who is too responsive or well-trained for the rider's capabilities. For example, reining has become one of the fastest-growing events. If you want to compete in this sport, buy a "starter" or "learner" horse who can do all of the maneuvers, but who is laid-back and easygoing.

If you buy a highly trained, extremely responsive horse who operates on a hair trigger, you will not be able to handle him. Riding him will not be fun or safe. It would be like giving a Ferrari to someone who can barely drive.

Here again, decide exactly what you want in your first horse, and do not overestimate your capabilities.

# Geldings, Mares, and Stallions

Your first horse should be a mare (a mature female horse) or a gelding, which is a castrated, or neutered, male. Stallions, or breeding age males, are not suitable for first-time horse owners. Some horsemen swear geldings are more reliable in disposition and attitude than mares.

Breeding-age mares do come "in season," usually every 21 days or so. During that time, one mare may handle and respond as she normally does; another may seem a little cranky and out of sorts, toward both the rider and/or other horses. However, some people contend that mares make more willing, responsive mounts, yet others consider that geldings are far steadier to handle and ride on a daily basis. The choice is yours.

Should your riding plans include another, more trained horse in the future, once you have mastered the basics of horsemanship, you may have considered the later possibility of raising a foal from your first horse. In that case, you know what you want—a mare. You aren't wasting time test-riding geldings.

However, if your interest is more in riding than raising horses, a gelding makes an equally good mount. Many people have no preference regarding mares and geldings as long as the horse performs in an acceptable manner.

# Size

Size is another consideration. A small child has a tougher time mounting an extremely large horse and appears out of proportion to his mount, just as a long-legged adult would look strange on an unusually short horse.

Generally speaking, small ponies do not make good mounts for children. They tend to have stubborn dispositions and are difficult for children to control. Because they are too small for an adult to ride and correct, the ponies continue to get away with doing whatever they want.

Another factor: The short stride of a small pony makes his gaits very choppy

*American Paint Horses are a colorful addition to any equine event. This one is used for posting the colors at a rodeo.*

11

*Here's a saddle-seat exhibitor on an Arabian horse.*

## Registered or Grade

In searching for a horse, you will hear the terms registered and grade. Some horses are registered with a particular breed association, as their parents were. The registration certificate lists the sire, or father, and the dam, or mother, of the horse, along with a physical description of the animal and a record of the previous owners.

The association, in addition to keeping the pedigree of a registered horse on file, also maintains a record of a horse's achievements in the show arena or on the racetrack in events approved or governed by the association's guidelines. When purchasing a registered horse, the registration certificate, along with a transfer of ownership and a fee, are sent to the association. The new owner later receives the certificate, which has been changed to show him as the horse's current owner.

On the other hand, grade is a term used to describe a horse not registered with a particular breed association, even though the horse may exhibit many characteristics of a certain breed. A grade horse can be from grade stock, with both sire and dam being considered grade animals, or can be parented by one grade horse, with the other parent being a registered horse. Any horse, no matter how typical he is of a particular breed, is known as a grade horse if registration papers are not available, for whatever reason.

Generally speaking, a registered horse is higher in price than a grade horse. If cost is a major factor to you and/or you don't plan to show in breed registry-approved events, a grade horse may suit you. There are many open events and activities for registered and grade horses alike. Should you later plan to sell your first horse, moving on to another mount, remember that a grade horse probably won't bring as high a resale price as a papered, or registered, horse will.

## Breeds

Horse breeds are defined by characteristics in conformation, color, gait, or a combination of these things. Most breed registries are willing to send prospective horse owners packets of information that

and uncomfortable. That can quickly discourage a child from riding.

When riding in a group, should a full-sized horse kick at a small pony, it's quite possible the horse will strike the child, rather than the pony. For this reason, many people prefer to start their children riding on larger horses. Larger ponies can make outstanding mounts for children. Several examples include the Welsh Pony, Welsh crosses, Quarter Ponies, and POAs.

Whatever the size of the rider and horse, look for balance in the picture you see during a test-ride. If the appearance is pleasing to the eye, the proportions of the horse and rider are probably appropriate.

*Endurance riding and Arabian horses seem to go hand-in-hand.*

**In recent years, however, the lines between English and western enthusiasts have become somewhat blurred.**

tell about the particular breed, the registry or association, and the programs and services offered. Pedigree searches, races, horse shows, youth and amateur activities, and award programs for ranch horses and trail horses are just a few of many possibilities. However, if you are familiar with a particular breed you prefer, you have narrowed the field of your search.

In recent years, the Quarter Horse, the Arabian and Half-Arabian, the Paint Horse, the Tennessee Walking Horse, and the Appaloosa have been among the most popular breeds.

The American Quarter Horse Association was organized in 1940, and the breed is the most popular in the country. The Quarter Horse is a versatile animal, performing capably in rodeo competition, racing, ranch work, show jumping, trail riding, and more. Standard gaits—the walk, trot, and canter—are performed by the breed, and the color of his coat can be one of many—sorrel, bay, black, gray, dun,

grulla, etc. A Quarter Horse may have white markings, but there are limits to how much white is acceptable for registration and/or breeding purposes.

Arabian pedigrees are maintained by the Arabian Horse Registry of America, and Half-Arabian pedigrees are maintained by the International Arabian Horse Association. Arabians have a long history and were exported from their native land many years ago, first to Europe and then to the United States. As with Quarter Horses, Arabians perform well in many riding activities. The most common coat colors in purebreds are gray, bay, chestnut, and black.

Although the Paint Horse is similar to the Quarter Horse in conformation and versatility, the Paint's most distinguishing

*People ride hunt-seat on many breeds of horses, including the Appaloosa, as shown here.*

feature is the color pattern of his coat. Usually it is a combination of white and another color in an irregular design of spots and splashes. The registry is the American Paint Horse Association.

Newcomers to the horse industry often confuse two terms—paint and pinto. The Paint Horse has standardized conformation and has been developed from Quarter Horse and Thoroughbred bloodlines. The Pinto has much the same coloration as the Paint, but can have bloodlines of any breed.

Appaloosas are known for a distinct color patterns as well. Among the most common is the leopard, which is white with black spots over the entire body. Another dominant color pattern is a spotted "blanket" on the horse's rump.

The Appaloosa Horse Club is the registry for this breed, which was used by the Nez Perce tribes of Idaho and Wash-ington. This is a color breed, and in recent years, Quarter Horse and Thoroughbred bloodlines have influenced Appaloosa breeding programs.

The Tennessee Walking Horse's gait is what sets him apart. The running walk is a smooth, comfortable gait and a ground-covering one as well, making this breed an obvious favorite among trail riders. The Walking Horse developed from a mixture of Morgan, Standardbred, Thoroughbred, and Saddlebred bloodlines in the southern part of the United States and can be found in a wide range of colors. Pedigrees are maintained by the Tennessee Walking Horse Breeders' and Exhibitors' Association.

## Riding Discipline

Once you have an idea of what type horse you would like to own, give some thought to what you plan to do with your horse. Do you plan to ride English or western? Many people practice both riding disciplines, often using the same horse to do both. Generally speaking, people develop more specific tastes in their choice of gear and horses as their level of riding experience increases, or, for example, if they target one event to compete in.

There are two popular styles of English riding—hunt-seat and saddle-seat. The tack, or equipment, is distinctly different from that used in western riding. Hunt-seat refers to the style of riding on hunters and jumpers, and saddle-seat describes the style of riding used on some gaited horses. In addition, riders practicing the different disciplines often wear distinct styles of clothing, more so in the show arena than for pleasure riding.

In recent years, however, the lines between English and western enthusiasts have become somewhat blurred. Horsemen now cross over from one riding discipline to another, ever seeking to increase their knowledge of and appreciation for horsemanship.

Beyond the style of riding, you also need to consider the type of riding you have in mind when you select your first horse. If pleasure riding or trail riding is your preference, again, the supply of horses from which to choose can be somewhat larger than if you are looking for a show horse or endurance riding horse.

Many people ride for pleasure in their own neighborhoods, seldom hauling their horses away from the home pasture. Other people enjoy trail rides organized by a local club. Some folks like nothing more than hauling their horses and tents or camper to the nearest forest or park area and hitting the trail there.

If you are competitive by nature, there's likely a riding club or horsemen's association that sponsors playdays or shows open to horses of any breed. Rodeo competition is open to young people of all ages and is often sanctioned by the National Little Britches Rodeo, the National High School Rodeo Association, or the National Intercollegiate Rodeo Association.

Youth and adults alike compete in open rodeos, and professional rodeo associations can be found at the state level. Nationwide, the Professional Rodeo Cowboys Association and the International Professional Rodeo Association, for example, approve events.

A variety of sport organizations, each devoted to a particular riding activity, abound. The United States Team Roping Championships, American Team Penning Championships, National Reining Horse Association, National Cutting Horse Association, North American Trail Ride Conference, and American Endurance Riding Conference are just a few of the many available options.

Not surprisingly, newcomers to the horse industry often get overloaded when they hit the information highway. There are so many choices that decision-making seems difficult, and all the newcomer wants to do is ride. As you search out your first horse, think in general terms at first, particularly if you are a novice rider.

# WHO CAN HELP YOU FIND YOUR HORSE

**2**

SUCCESS in finding a suitable first horse is not always a case of what you know, but who you know. Networking—contacting horsemen you know and getting word of your search out to those you don't know—is important when you're looking for a horse.

One place to start your search is by spending a little time with the best horseman you know. If you have been riding long enough to want to become a horse owner, likely you have become acquainted with some horsemen in your area, either personally or by reputation. When you choose a top horseman to help in your search, listen to the advice he or she gives. He didn't reach his level of accomplishment by deciding he knew all about horses before he bought the first one.

Most horsemen are enthusiastic about their sport and don't mind talking about horses and horsemanship at all. If the best horseman you know is a friend, that's good. Ask if he or she would mind giving you a little guidance in your search for a horse. You probably won't pay a friend for

*Check local riding club bulletin boards to find out who has what for sale.*

16

his time, in this case, unless he is in the business of giving riding lessons or training horses. But don't forget to show a little appreciation for his effort by buying lunch or filling his truck with gas if necessary.

If, by reputation, you know of an equine industry professional in your area, don't be afraid to call him for a consultation. After all, he is in the horse business, in one respect or another, and it's doubtful that you are the first to call with such a request. Do remember, however, that this is his business, and be willing to pay for his time. Some professionals don't mind giving you an hour or so of their time; they figure that eventually you might have need of the goods or services they offer once you do become a horse owner.

Whether it's a friend or professional, consider the best horseman you know a voice of reason in your search for a first horse. A good horseman can help assess your level of riding ability with the riding

goals you have in mind. The more riding experience this person has had, the more likely it is that he can offer you some guidelines on a horse suitable for what you want to do. In addition, a longtime horseman simply knows more people in the area who might have a horse for the first-time owner.

To make the most of the time you spend with another horseman, be honest with him. Let him know what you want in a

*Stables often have many horses available for sale. Be sure, however, that you're not buying someone else's problem.*

17

Networking among local riding instructors and their students is a good way to begin the search for your first horse.

If you have an outfitter in your area, check with him. He may have a really broke horse who is, perhaps, too old to continue hitting the trail, but who might serve well as your first horse.

*Clinics are an excellent place to gather information about instructors, trainers, and horses.*

horse, what you can afford to spend on a horse, and what you'll do in exchange for his help. By the same token, he should be honest with you. If there is an hourly fee for his time or a finder's fee involved in the search, he should be straightforward about it.

If a prospective first horse standing in his barn is not his own, it's possible he is selling the horse on a commission basis for the owner. That's okay if the horseman helping you is interested in having your business later down the line. As a result, he wants to ensure that you find a good mount. But it also could be that he's more interested in making a fast buck by selling you a horse, whether it's a suitable mount or not.

The longstanding rule of thumb in a horse trade of any sort: Let the buyer be-

**If you see a horse who catches your eye at a club activity, seek out the owner and let him know you're interested. Many people, when looking for a child's first mount, know exactly what they want— a horse just like the one a child in the local club has been riding.**

*If you have a particular type of riding in mind, such as roping, attend a local rodeo or jackpot. Observe the action and ask questions to learn more about both the event and the horsemen there.*

ware. If you know the horseman helping you, you likely know something of his ability and his ethics. If you don't know him, try to find out something about him from a horseman you do know and have confidence in. Consider how long a professional has been in business in your area. It shouldn't be too difficult to find someone who has taken lessons from him, had a horse trained by him, or bought or sold a horse through his barn. It's possible the pro himself will be willing to give you the name of a satisfied customer or two. If you are paying for his time, this is not an unreasonable request.

In addition to letting your friends and professional horsemen in the area know you are looking for a horse to buy, go to the places that horsemen frequent—feed stores, veterinarian offices, and riding stables. Often there is a bulletin board for use by people who want to buy or sell horses. Read the classified advertisements in your local newspaper. Even though a horse being advertised may not be what you want, the owner may know of another horse who might fit your requirements.

Join a local riding club and attend the meetings, shows, and activities. Speak up and let people know you're ready to buy. If you see a horse who catches your eye at a club activity, seek out the owner and let him know you're interested. Many people, when looking for a child's first mount, know exactly what they want—a horse just like the one a child in the local club has been riding. If that's the case, go to the

*A farrier makes regular visits to area horse barns, so he's often among the first to know when a horse becomes available for purchase. Don Baskins, Tucumcari, N.M., shoes at barns in a five-state area.*

parents and let them know of your interest and how to contact you. The horse may not be for sale now, but 2 months later, the situation could change.

Many horsemen, amateur riders and professionals alike, don't mind passing along information about horses for sale or about prospective purchasers looking to buy. But that won't happen until people know you are looking for a horse.

# WHAT TO LOOK FOR WHEN YOU SHOP

## 3

WHEN YOU shop for a first horse, look at the horse's conformation, the structure and form of his body. Does he appear balanced in build, or does a part of his body lack symmetry and seem out of place with the rest? A problem in conformation often shows in the way a horse travels. And a problem in a horse's way of going could result in lameness and severely curtail the actual riding time you get in the saddle.

The form of the horse's body should function or serve the purpose for which

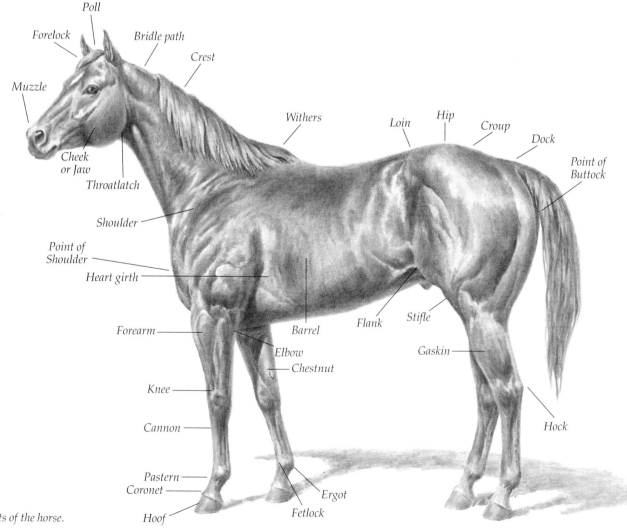

*The parts of the horse.*

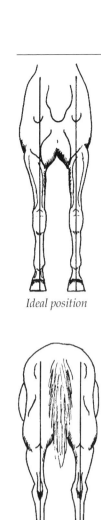

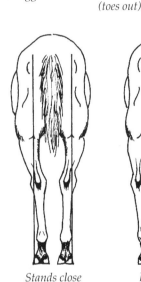

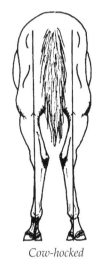
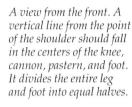

| *Ideal position* | *Toes out* | *Bowlegged* | *Narrow-chested (toes out)* | *Base narrow (stands close)* | *Knock-kneed* | *Pigeon-toed* |

*A view from the front. A vertical line from the point of the shoulder should fall in the centers of the knee, cannon, pastern, and foot. It divides the entire leg and foot into equal halves.*

| *Ideal position* | *Stands wide* | *Stands close* | *Bowlegged* | *Cow-hocked* |

BILL CULBERTSON © 1987

*The hind legs from the rear. A vertical line from the point of the buttock should fall in the centers of the hock, cannon, pastern, and foot.*

**Illustrations by Bill Culbertson, Emeritus Livestock Extension Specialist, courtesy of Ann Swinker, Ph.D., Extension Horse Specialist, Colorado State University.**

the horse will be used. The more demanding your riding plans are, the greater, usually, the effects of a conformational problem can become. A well-built horse can withstand the physical demands of high-level competition for a longer time than can a poorly built animal.

No matter whether you're evaluating a cutting prospect, who is apt to have a small and compact build, or a jumper, who is somewhat taller and rangier in build, look for symmetry and balance in how the horse is physically put together. There is no perfect horse, just as there is no perfect rider. Generally speaking, however, there are plenty of serviceable horses around, capable of carrying you well into your newfound sport. A look at what is desirable in a horse gives you a basis for comparison as you view prospects for purchase.

# Feet and Legs

Study a prospect from the ground up. The four hoofs and legs support the horse's body weight, along with the additional weight of the rider and saddle. Think of the horse's leg, from the fetlock up to his body, as a column of bones. The straighter and more well-aligned the parts of the column are, the better the column supports what is overhead.

Since you are purchasing a horse to ride, this is the function you want his form to provide—ridability. A major conformational problem in the feet or legs makes a horse unsuitable for riding.

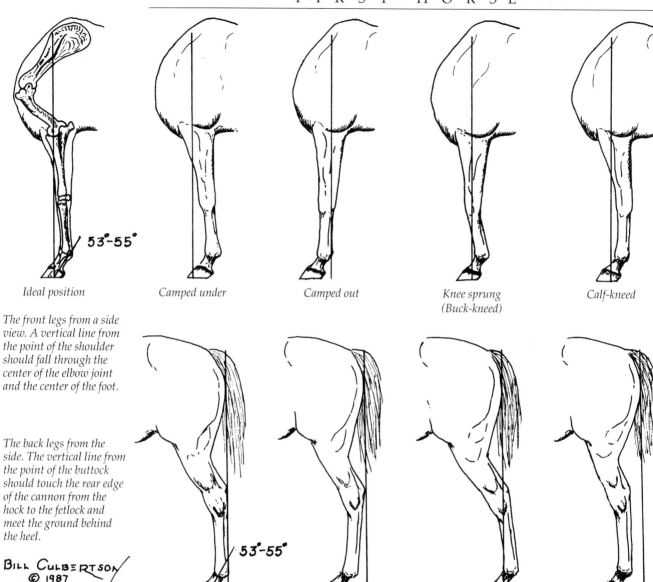

*Ideal position*

*Camped under*

*Camped out*

*Knee sprung (Buck-kneed)*

*Calf-kneed*

The front legs from a side view. A vertical line from the point of the shoulder should fall through the center of the elbow joint and the center of the foot.

The back legs from the side. The vertical line from the point of the buttock should touch the rear edge of the cannon from the hock to the fetlock and meet the ground behind the heel.

BILL CULBERTSON
© 1987

**Illustrations by Bill Culbertson, Emeritus Livestock Extension Specialist, courtesy of Ann Swinker, Ph.D., Extension Horse Specialist, Colorado State University.**

*Ideal position*

*Stands under*

*Camped out*

*Post-legged (Leg too straight)*

Look at a horse from the front, the side, and the back. Drop imaginary plumb lines to the ground to determine straightness. The accompanying illustrations show good conformation in the horse, as well as some of the more common defects.

## Profile

Viewed from the side, a horse's top line should be shorter than his underline, to help ensure a longer, more balanced stride. A long back is not as strong, either. Nor is an extremely short-backed horse desirable; he might have a short, choppy stride and therefore ride rougher than a better balanced horse.

The top line and the underline, combined with the angle of the shoulder and

24

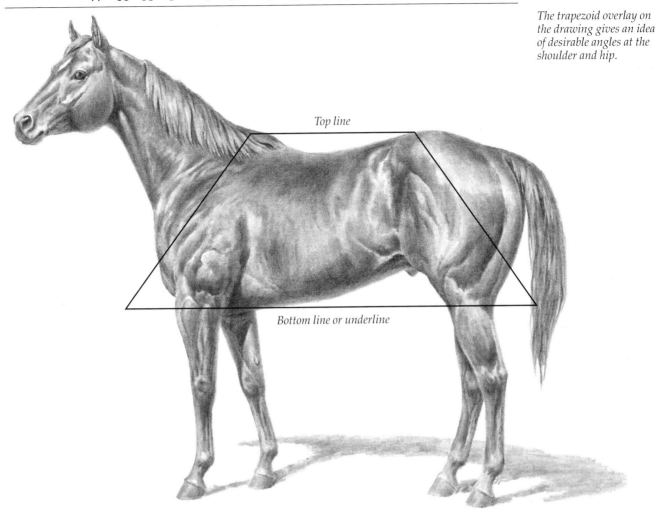

*Top line*

*Bottom line or underline*

*The trapezoid overlay on the drawing gives an idea of desirable angles at the shoulder and hip.*

the angle of the hip, make up a trapezoid, the geometric form often used to describe balance in conformation. Look for matching angles at the hip and shoulder. If the trapezoid formed is a balanced one, the horse is probably well-balanced in his conformation.

## Head and Neck

Because a horse uses his neck and head for balance, both should be proportionate to his body. Again, balance is the key. One rule of thumb calls for the length of the neck, from the poll to the withers, to be about the same as the distance from the withers to the croup. Another rule of thumb suggests that the length of the neck on top, along the crest, should be about twice as long as the underline of the neck.

## Blemishes and Unsoundnesses

When looking at a prospect, understand the difference between a blemish and an unsoundness. A blemish, such as an unsightly scar, may detract from a horse's appearance, but doesn't affect the usefulness or serviceability of the animal. An unsoundness, on the other hand, is a problem that does affect how useful a horse can be. Such is the case with a parrot-mouthed (overbite) horse who has difficulty grazing, or a horse with a bog spavin or bowed tendon.

*Unsoundnesses and blemishes.*

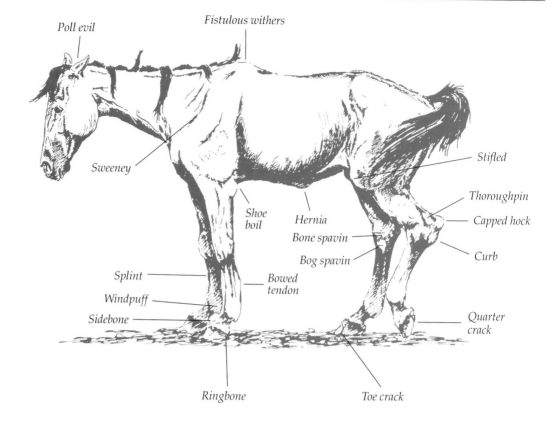

Illustration by Bill Culbertson, Emeritus Livestock Extension Specialist, courtesy of Ann Swinker, Ph.D., Extension Horse Specialist, Colorado State University.

How large a problem a conformational fault, unsoundness, or blemish in a horse creates for the rider depends primarily on two things: how severe the fault is and how demanding the rider is of the horse.

You'll likely hear the term "serviceably sound" during your search for a horse. This term describes an animal with a problem or flaw of some kind, but whose performance is considered acceptable, or serviceable, to the rider. The problem may limit the horse's usefulness somewhat, but has not rendered the animal totally useless.

# Parts of the Horse

**Hoof:** The horn-like covering over a horse's foot should be fairly smooth in appearance. Obvious rings running around the hoof, or a somewhat bumpy appearance, can be indicative of a previous problem such as founder. A quarter crack or toe crack is a vertical split in the horse's hoof and is not desirable.

**Coronet:** The coronet runs around the upper portion of the hoof wall, where the hoof ends and hair begins. A blow to the coronet can result in irregular hoof growth, just as with a human when a blow to the base of a fingernail results in irregular nail growth. A sidebone, which can lead to unsoundness, is a hard enlargement found on the side or to the rear of the foot, where coronet and hoof join.

**Pastern:** The slope of the pastern should should roughly correspond with the slope of the hoof and the slope of the shoulder.

This is important as a horse supports about two-thirds of his body weight on the two front legs; any misalignment here creates undue strain.

Pasterns too straight result in increased concussion when the feet hit the ground. This can predispose a horse to unsoundness in the hoofs. Too, a straight-pasterned horse usually rides rougher. Although offering a smoother ride, too long a slope in the pastern also creates strain on the horse since the weight-bearing bones of the lower leg are not well-aligned over the foot.

A ringbone is a hard growth found on the bones in the pastern and is an unsoundness.

**Fetlock:** This joint should have a clean, somewhat smooth appearance. A soft swollen area, a windpuff, may indicate that the fetlock has been strained from overuse.

**Ergot:** The horny growth found on the fetlock joint. Excessive growth here can be twisted off or cut with scissors.

**Cannon:** The cannon bones, both front and rear, should be relatively short in comparison to the upper leg, and straight, to create less strain on ligaments and tendons. Viewed from the side, the cannon gives a broad, flat appearance because of the tendon running along the back of the bone. When stressed severely, this tendon can become bowed, or strained.

Splints are small bony growths usually found on the inside of the cannon bone and often develop as a result of stress or from a blow. A curb is a hard swelling found on the rear cannon, below the hock.

**Knee:** The knee should be broad and somewhat flat in appearance when viewed from the front and, when viewed from the side, should have enough depth to appear proportionate to the other bones in the leg. Viewed from either direction, the knee should be well-aligned between the upper and lower leg.

**Chestnut:** The horny growth on the inside of a horse's legs. Excessive growth here can be peeled away, or carefully cut away with scissors.

**Forearm:** The muscling on the upper portion of the front leg should look long and smooth. Ideal muscling is said to "tie in well at the knee," or taper deeply into the knee.

**Hock:** When viewed from the side, the hock should be wide in appearance. The point of the hock is the prominent angle giving shape to the back leg.

A capped hock occurs when the point of the hock has become enlarged. A bog spavin is found on the inner part of the hock and is softer than a bone spavin, a hard growth on the lower part of the hock. Puffiness above the hock is called a thoroughpin.

**Gaskin:** Both inside and outside gaskin muscles above the hock should be long, tying into the hock smoothly and deeply, or low, on the hock.

**Stifle:** When a horse is described as stifled, this joint has been displaced.

**Barrel:** A well-sprung rib cage gives roundness to a horse's barrel, in addition to providing ample room for organs such as the lungs. Good lung capacity means a stronger, more enduring horse, so depth in the barrel, through the heart girth, from the withers to the underline, is desirable.

**Flank:** Horses are somewhat ticklish in the flank area, between the rib and hip. The flank should taper smoothly into the hindquarters. A wasp-waisted horse has a flank that tapers high into the hindquarters.

**Head:** Depth of mouth is often considered indicative of how responsive a horse is to training. In other words, a light-mouthed horse often is shallow in the mouth. However, any horse's responsiveness is directly related to the rider's use of the reins and bit.

Teeth affect how well or how poorly a horse utilizes his food. Ascertain that the

**Many horsemen can determine a horse's age by looking at his teeth, but it takes time to master the technique.**

upper and lower teeth match, with no evidence of an overbite called a parrot mouth, or an underbite. Many horsemen can determine a horse's age by looking at his teeth, but it takes time to master the technique.

Large nostrils enable the horse to take in plenty of oxygen to better withstand the demands of physical labor. Pay particular attention to any breathing difficulties; a roaring or heaving sound may be indicative of lung damage.

From muzzle to forelock the head should be relatively straight and smooth although "dish" faces are desirable in Arabians. A Roman-nosed horse, convex from the eyes to muzzle, is considered unattractive. Any severe bumps on the head between the eyes and nostrils could indicate overuse of severe head-setting devices.

**Eyes:** Wide-set eyes enable a horse to better see what is going on around him, and go hand-in-hand with a broad forehead, also an appealing feature. Horsemen often speak of large, quiet eyes as desirable. This is not the case with a pig-eyed horse, for example, who has smaller, less appealing eyes. Should a horse's eye appear white or blue, rather than brown with a black pupil, he is described as glass-eyed. Glass eyes have no effect on vision, but a cloudy eye should be checked by a veterinarian.

**Ears:** These should be well-set and proportionate to a horse's head for maximum appeal. Ears that don't point forward, are set more on the side of the head than the top, or are overly long are functional, but are not as attractive.

**Throatlatch:** Horsemen speak of a clean throatlatch as being a desirable one. A refined throatlatch is preferred. Too thick a throatlatch makes it difficult for a horse to breathe well when he flexes at the poll, important in training a responsive horse who can perform well.

**Shoulder:** Sloping shoulders, often referred to as "laid-back," allow for a long stride, which is confortable to ride. The angle of the shoulder corresponds to a line drawn from the withers to the point of the shoulder. Too steep or straight an angle leads to a shorter stride and rougher ride. Note that the straighter shoulder negates the balance and symmetry in the previously described trapezoid.

**Withers:** The withers, at the end of the horse's neck, rise slightly over the shoulders before tapering into the back. If the withers are too high, you'll likely have trouble properly fitting a saddle to the horse. Too low, or mutton-withered, and it's difficult to keep a saddle properly positioned; it tends to roll. The height of the withers should balance with the height of the horse at the croup. When the croup is higher than the withers, it's difficult to properly fit a saddle to the horse, and results in a "downhill" feeling for the rider.

**Loin:** The loin couples the back to the hindquarters. The shorter the loin, generally, the more strength it has, better enabling a horse to utilize the powerful drive of his hindquarters by drawing them well under his body. A loin too long is not as strong and sometimes develops soreness after a strenuous workout.

**Hip:** The points of a horse's hips are prominent areas on either side of the loin. When viewed from behind, these points should balance horizontally. When viewed from the side, the angle of the hip measures from the point of the hip to the point of the

**When the points of conformation are tied together in a moving package, the result is known as a horse's way of going.**

buttocks. A well-balanced horse has matching shoulder and hip angles.

**Croup:** Ideally, the croup should not fall off too steeply toward the tail.

# Way of Going

Looking at a horse is one thing; seeing the animal in action is another. When the points of conformation are tied together in a moving package, the result is known as a horse's way of going, no matter what the gait or speed of travel. The walk, trot, and lope are rhythmic gaits, each with a distinctive beat and pattern.

The walk is a four-beat gait, with each foot leaving the ground independently of the other three. You should be able to count four even, regular beats. If you can't, there is a problem causing this irregularity; possibly the horse is lame. Although the walk is slow in speed, about 4 miles per hour, the horse's way of going should be straight, with his body well-aligned, and should show a sense of purpose and direction in movement.

The trot is known as a diagonal gait since the horse's right fore and left hind strike the ground together, as do the left fore and right hind. Obviously, the trot is a two-beat gait. Sometimes called a jog or jog-trot when performed slowly, the gait can be performed fast—called a long trot—with the horse fully extending his stride.

The lope is a three-beat gait and has somewhat of a diagonal movement since a foreleg and the opposite hind leg strike the ground simultaneously. The other front leg is the leading leg, hence the term lead, which is used to describe a horse's movement, depending on the direction of travel.

For example, a horse loping to the right strikes the ground first with his left hind foot. The diagonal pair, the right hind and left foreleg, strike the ground at the same time—beat number two. The third beat of the gait occurs when the right foreleg strikes the ground. The opposite is true for a horse loping in the left lead—

right hind, left hind and right front, and left front.

The important thing about a lead in the lope: By taking the correct lead for a given direction of travel, the horse's movement is more balanced and efficient for a top performance.

Although the way of going can vary somewhat among different breeds of horses used for different purposes, any horse's motion should be straightforward and well-coordinated. If his feet move more laterally than straight, his action is probably less coordinated or less efficient and, possibly, less comfortable to ride. Horsemen use a number of terms to describe less than ideal action.

Forging or scalping, for example, describes what happens when a horse strikes a forefoot with the toe of a hind foot. Horses who are somewhat narrow between the front legs and/or splay-footed are more prone to interfere, or strike the cannon bone or fetlock of one leg with the other. Paddling or winging out occurs when the foot action travels out to the side, rather than following a straightforward path. A horse cross-fires when a hind foot interferes with the action of the diagonal forefoot.

**Horsemen use a number of terms to describe less than ideal action.**

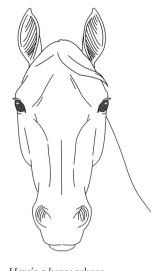

*A threatening, aggressive expression is usually accompanied by pinned ears.*

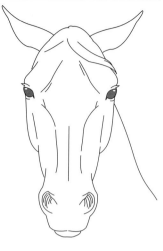

*This horse is somewhat drowsy or relaxed.*

*Here's a horse whose attention is focused. He has an alert, responsive expression.*

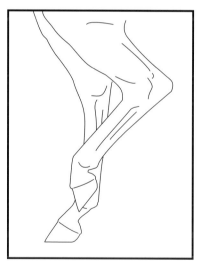

*You can tell somewhat where a horse's attenton is focused by watching his ears work. If he works his ears quickly, from front to back, it could indicate that he is uneasy in his present position.*

## First Impressions

Beyond considering a horse's conformation and his way of going when you look at a prospect, give some thought to the initial impression a horse creates. Are his ears pinned? Are his teeth bared as if he would like to bite? Does he threaten to kick with a back leg when approached in the stall or pen? Is his expression alert and interested, or a bored one? Does he seem frightened, or appear aggressive instead? Or does he give the impression that he holds his handler in high regard, respecting the human's territory and being responsive to his commands?

These general impressions give you something of an idea of a horse's attitude toward people and other horses. It is acceptable for one horse within a herd to threaten another by kicking; that's his way of maintaining the social order in the herd. It is not, however, acceptable for any horse to threaten a handler when he approaches.

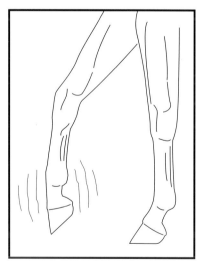

*A horse demonstrates impatience, often at feeding time, by pawing with his front leg.*

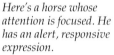

*A raised back leg means a horse feels threatened and has become defensive, preparing to kick.*

# Ask Questions

Inquire about the horse's previous health care. A following chapter is devoted to that subject, but you need to be aware of the horse's deworming and shoeing schedule, along with any floating that may have been done to his teeth.

Ask how current the horse's vaccinations are, as well as his Coggins test. Some equine vaccinations, such as for tetanus or sleeping sickness, are routine nationwide; others, such as the one for Potomac fever, may be necessary only in certain geographic areas. A Coggins test determines if a horse is a carrier of equine infectious anemia. It is required for most interstate travel and for entry at sale barns, show grounds, or organized trail rides.

If you have determined that a particular prospect is the horse for you, consider having a veterinarian make a pre-purchase examination of the horse. A veterinarian is not a psychic; he cannot tell you what the horse's health or soundness will be a month from now. He can, however, give you an idea of the horse's current state of health, possibly pointing out a potential problem that you, as a layman, would not be aware of. And a routine check could well give you peace of mind in making the purchase.

A routine or minor pre-purchase check includes checking that the horse's temperature, pulse, respiration, gut sounds, and way of going are within normal levels. The veterinarian can check the horse's teeth as well to see if they need to be "floated," or filed more evenly, to get maximum benefit from his feed. Should you decide to purchase the animal, this is an ideal time to have a fresh Coggins test and administer any necessary vaccinations.

If you plan to pursue a particularly strenuous activity with your first horse, you might opt to have a major pre-purchase examination performed. Again, the veterinarian cannot foresee the future, but he can better determine how well-suited a horse is for a specific purpose, such as dressage or roping.

Major examinations are more costly and can include X-rays and further lab-testing. However, many people purchasing high-dollar horses, particularly for competitive purposes, find that the expense of a major examination is well worth it.

Don't feel discouraged at this point, thinking there is far more to know about horses than you'll ever learn. The more horses you see, the better an eye you often develop for the finer points of conformation, along with the more common unsoundnesses or blemishes. That's why it's good to have a top horseman helping in the search for your first horse. A good horseman can take a lot of the mystery out of conformation by using a real horse in a demonstration, rather than an illustration on the page.

**If you have determined that a particular prospect is the horse for you, consider having a veterinarian make a pre-purchase examination of the horse.**

# HOW TO TEST-RIDE YOUR HORSE

**4**

ONCE YOU decide that a horse among the prospects you've seen is pleasing in appearance and seems healthy and sound for the type riding you have in mind, it's time for a test-ride. Before you jump astride the horse, take a few moments to notice some things that might help you decide if this prospect is the best first horse for you.

Since you have already determined that he's worthy of a test-ride, you've probably seen the owner handle the horse, to an extent, from the ground. Were you, however, present when the horse was caught in the pasture or approached in the stall? If so, did the horse turn his hindquarters to the handler in a threatening way, or did the horse face up, acknowledging the handler as someone worthy of respect? Could the handler easily halter the horse, or was it a troublesome process? If you didn't actually see these things that are part of an everyday riding routine, do so at some point.

Notice how well the horse leads from the ground. Does he willingly follow alongside the handler, maintaining a respectful distance? Or does he lag back,

*Be sure you can catch any horse you are considering for purchase.*

tugging against the lead rope, or try to rush ahead of the handler, crowding him? When the handler comes to a halt, is the horse responsive? Does he follow the handler's lead when asked to turn both ways as he is being led?

Ask the handler if the horse will longe, circling the handler at the end of a long line. If a horse can be longed, the handler probably will volunteer the information and offer to demonstrate. He may snap a long line or rope—the longe line—into the horse's halter, or he may turn the horse loose in a round pen and free-longe him. Either way, a horse who longes can be an asset to you, particularly if you are a novice horseman.

Longeing is an excellent way to warm up a horse in preparation for a ride, and it helps you develop a rapport with your new companion. The horse who learns to respect you when you're afoot will be more apt to respect you once you're mounted. In addition, longeing is excellent for the horse who has been stalled for a few days without regular exercise, or for the one who is feeling extra energetic due to a change in the weather. Longeing can help bring a horse's energy level to more manageable proportions in these cases and helps decrease the risk factor, especially for an inexperienced rider.

When the handler longes the horse, study his responsiveness. The horse should hold a circle well, not angling in toward the handler in smaller and smaller circles. When the handler says whoa, the horse should stop. This gives you an idea of how well he will respond to whoa when you're riding him.

After any longeing demonstration, take note of how the horse responds to the handler during the grooming and saddling process. The horse should stand quietly while his head, body, and legs are being brushed. Ask the handler to clean the horse's feet, both front and rear. Again, these are everyday things to a broke horse accustomed to being handled regularly.

When the horse is being brushed and saddled is also a good time to ask if he tolerates clippers being used to trim his ears or bridle path. Don't be afraid to ask for a demonstration. Horses who are trimmed only on the occasional basis likely won't be as accepting of the process as those who have been clipped and trimmed on a regular basis. However, whatever the

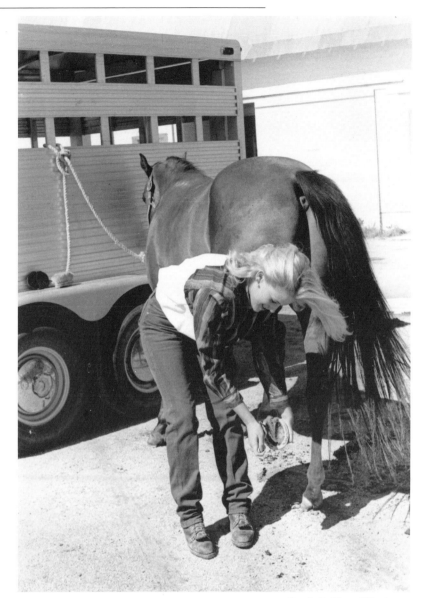

*Sarah Pulliam, Elbert, Colo., demonstrates cleaning a horse's hoof. You should be able to handle your horse's feet, both front and rear.*

horse's level of acceptance, it must be one that you feel adequate to deal with. Again, if this is unfamiliar territory, rely on the horseman with you; he can help evaluate whether clipping is likely to become more of a problem for you. A little patience and desensitizing of the horse can make clipping less of a problem.

*It's good to know that a prospect can tolerate having his bridle path clipped.*

As the handler prepares to saddle the horse, notice his reaction when the blanket is placed on his back. He should accept it quietly. The same holds true when the saddle, with all the dangling gear, is put on the horse's back. When the cinch is tightened, the horse should accept it, and not pin his ears or threaten to bite the handler.

Pay particular attention when the handler bridles the horse. Is the horse head-shy and fussy about having his ears handled? A hard-to-bridle horse can be difficult to cope with.

Now, too, is the time to ask any questions you may have about a particular bit being used on the horse. Your horseman friend can be of real help here, especially if you don't feel you have a good understanding of bits. Should the handler comment that the horse will ride with almost any bit in his mouth, ask for a demonstration.

If the handler puts a tie-down on the horse, question the need for it. The horse could be a real head-slinger, or the handler could team rope or barrel race regularly and use the tie-down for competition. It could be unnecessary for everyday pleasure riding.

Remember: The only dumb question, at this point in searching for your first horse, is the one you failed to ask.

The handler should ride the horse first and demonstrate what the horse can do. If the handler will not ride the horse, be very wary. In fact, it's best to move on and look at another horse. Watch closely to determine what cues the handler uses to get the response he wants from the horse. If you are mystified by how the handler cues the horse for a maneuver, ask for another demonstration and an explanation.

Ideally, the horse should stand quietly for you to mount and remain still until you ask him to move out. By using the same cues as the handler, you should be able to walk, trot, and lope the horse straight and in circles, both to the left and to the right. In addition, the horse should be consistent in each of the three gaits, whether he's traveling on the straight-away or in a circle. The horse should willingly rate his speed when asked, slowing from a canter to a trot, or stopping completely, without fighting the bit. Making a

*Your first horse shouldn't object to having his ears handled.*

*Will the prospect stand quietly for mounting?*

**The degree of finesse you expect as the horse performs different maneuvers depends, somewhat, on what you plan to do with the horse.**

turn in either direction should be easily accomplished. When you dismount, again, the horse should stand still.

Notice if the horse seems willing to perform under saddle. Is his expression a pleasant one, or are his ears pinned back, indicating obvious ill temper? Does the horse willingly move out on command, or does he appear balky or unwilling to leave the barn? When the handler asks the horse to execute a turn, does the horse do so, or does he turn his head in the other direction in obvious resentment of the pressure from the bit? Watch closely when the handler asks the horse to back. Does he step back actively, or is he sluggish, forcing the rider to drag him back? Is there complete resistance, accompanied by head-tossing or a threat of rearing?

Whoa means stop—dead-still—and stand there. It does not mean to slow to another gait, from a lope to a walk, for example. Whoa means stop—right now. Does the horse stop on command?

The degree of finesse you expect as the horse performs different maneuvers depends, somewhat, on what you plan to do with the horse. The finer points are more important, for example, if you are an experienced amateur rider expecting to enter non-pro reining competition. On the other hand, if you plan to pleasure ride, multiple 360-degree turnarounds may not be high on your priority list. If you are a pleasure rider with a strong interest in improving your horsemanship, a horse offering a middle-of-the-road response to cues may well be one you can work with and even improve as your horsemanship ability grows.

Accepting a first horse who is not highly trained is okay, and that horse can deliver a great deal of riding pleasure. Do not, however, be accepting of a first horse who is extremely ill-tempered or strongly resistant to the most basic commands—no matter how gorgeous the horse may be or how eye-catching his color.

Once you have seen the prospective first horse under saddle, it's time to mount up. Be honest with the handler about your level of expertise. There is nothing wrong with not knowing the fine points of horsemanship; it is wrong to compromise your own safety and that of the horse and those around you by professing to be something you are not—an experienced horseman. The owner will be all the more willing to help you have a successful ride when your honesty suggests you are willing to listen to and learn from him.

If there's a choice between riding in an open field or an enclosed arena, ride in the arena first. Give yourself and the horse the opportunity to show one another what each is capable of. Once you are satisfied that the lines of communication are open, there's plenty of time to test-ride the horse in the open.

Listen attentively as you mount up; do as the handler instructs. Take your time when test-riding, doing one thing at a time until you are satisfied that the horse is under control. While walking, stop and turn the horse periodically. Then, progress to a trot, again stopping and turning occasionally to check your control.

When you are ready to lope, cue the horse correctly, particularly if the handler has demonstrated that the horse will take either lead. Follow the handler's advice.

Should neither you nor the horse have a real understanding of leads, don't despair. Many people have spent many pleasant hours trail and pleasure riding, without giving a thought to the proper lead. Again, the purpose for which you are purchasing a horse directly affects what you find acceptable in a horse's performance. Throughout the test-ride, notice if the horse willingly moves out on command and if he stops on command. Don't ask him to stop or turn in the same place each

*Once you're comfortable riding a horse in a pen or arena, don't neglect to check out how well he responds in an open area.*

time; horses are creatures of habit and quickly learn to anticipate a routine. Do ask him to turn both ways and travel in both directions. See if he rates well, going from a faster gait to a slower one, and vice versa, with ease. These maneuvers are reflections of the control the rider has over the horse. Control is the foremost consideration in ensuring your personal safety when you ride. For a novice rider, a feeling of control and safety opens the door for developing the confidence to truly enjoy the sport of riding.

Once you are satisfied that you can control the horse and perform basic maneuvers, don't be afraid to ask the horse for any additional maneuvers you saw the handler request previously. Granted, your horsemanship skills may not be as good as the handler's, but you will learn some things about the horse, particularly how tolerant he is of rider error. This is especially important for a novice rider, who will make mistakes that the horse will be expected to handle with good grace.

If you make a mistake in cueing the horse, for example, and he doesn't get rattled and tries to respond correctly, you have likely found a good mount for an inexperienced horseman. If, however, the horse becomes extremely uneasy when you make a mistake, openly resisting a pull on the bit or dancing on his feet, unable to quietly go about his business of responding to the rider's cues, seriously question if this is the horse for you.

Do remember that, in such a situation, the first few mistakes you make during the test-ride are probably the most difficult ones for you and the horse to overcome. Don't panic and don't hurry. This is not the time for an emotional runaway on your part to add to the confusion; it's time to take a businesslike approach toward reestablishing the lines of communication. If you have the riding experience to correct the problem, that's great. If you don't, in a matter-of-fact way ask the handler what to do to rectify the situation. Then, take your time and do it.

*If you plan on trail riding a lot, be sure the horse can handle a water crossing.*

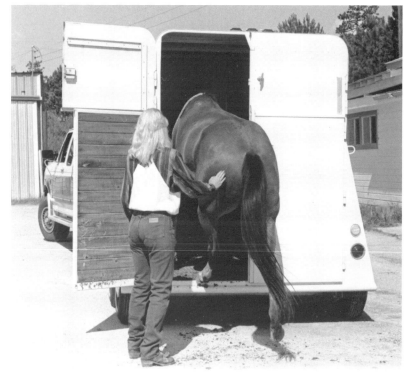

*Don't buy a horse until you're sure he will load into a trailer. A two-horse side-by-side is the ultimate test. Most horses load more easily into a slant-load or a stock-type trailer.*

Often, when you test-ride a horse, the handler will say, "Ride him like he's yours." That means to ride the horse as if you own him. Ride him with a feeling of confidence; you ask him to perform, and you expect him to respond appropriately. Don't worry if you err in performing a maneuver; maintain the horse's respect, above all. You may realize you have given a command incorrectly, and the horse may well be confused by it. You have, however, told him to do something, so insist that the horse make some effort to do something, however poor the result. Or simply say whoa, stop, and try the maneuver again. By maintaining the horse's respect, you give yourself the opportunity to immediately try a maneuver again in a more correct way, with much less confusion to both you and the horse.

In addition to test-riding a prospect, there are additional questions to ask when considering a horse for purchase. Don't accept a glib answer from the handler; ask him to demonstrate that the horse can do these things.

Breed __ANDALUSIAN__ Age __10__

Color __GREY__ Approx. wgt. __1000__

Used for __PLEASURE/TRAIL__ Sex __GELD__

Brand Inspector __ELDON CROWDER__

№ 35652

This permit void when horse changes ownership and must be returned to State Board of Stock Inspection by the holder.

This permit issued in compliance with section 35-53-129, 1973 Colorado Session Laws and must accompany horse at all times when in transit.

COLORADO DEPARTMENT OF AGRICULTURE
State Board of Stock Inspection
201 Livestock Exchange Bldg.
Denver, Colorado 80216
HORSE TRANSPORTATION PERMIT

Date Issued __JUNE 26__ 19 __90__

Owner __KATHY KADASH & RICK SWAN__

Address __3320 BEECHWOOD COURT__

City __COLO SPRGS__ State __CO 80918__

State Board of Stock Inspection

Brand Commissioner

NAME: __MISS MINDY'S DOT__

TATTOO: _____

REG. NO.: __21012__

NO BRAND

1/ Will the horse load into a two-horse trailer? Many horses who will load into a more open, stock-type trailer hesitate to enter a more cave-like, enclosed two-horse trailer. Although you may not own a trailer, there will be times when you must haul your horse somewhere—a trip to the veterinarian's office, for example. For more information, see the chapter on hauling.

2/ Will he cross water? This is an important consideration for a horse to be used for trail riding.

3/ Is the horse easy to catch in the pasture?

4/ Does the horse have such undesirable habits as stall weaving, cribbing, or wood chewing?

When it is all said and done, and your test-ride is over, take a few moments for evaluation. Realistically assess the horse's abilities for the riding you have in mind. Do you think he will serve the purpose? Without flinching, consider the true measure of your own abilities and how they stack up in relation to the horse.

Did the test-ride leave you feeling good, thinking of all the possibilities you can enjoy with this horse? Or did you feel uneasy, not quite in control of things? Or does "I love his neat head, his color, his long tail, etc.," scream in your mind while "I'm not too sure about this" whispers in

the background? Buying a horse for looks is fine, if that's all you plan to do—look at him.

For the first-time horse owner who is also a relatively inexperienced rider, actions speak louder than looks. Is the level of the horse's ability compatible with your level of riding ability? In other words, the two of you should make a team and complement one another.

If you feel you do, get out your checkbook—you've found your first horse.

A word of caution: When you purchase a horse, treat the purchase just as you would that of any other major item. Get a bill of sale, along with proof of a current Coggins test. A current health certificate

**All too often a buyer is told a horse is registered, "but my uncle has the certificate."**

*A registration certificate identifies the owners of a horse, both past and present, and the horse by his markings.*

Certificate of Registration

# AMERICAN QUARTER HORSE ASSOCIATION
### Amarillo, Texas 79168

| NAME | | REGISTRATION NUMBER | STATE FOALED |
|---|---|---|---|
| POCOS DIAMOND ROSE | | 3280593 | COLORADO |

| COLOR | SEX | FOALED | |
|---|---|---|---|
| RED DUN | MARE | MARCH 31, 1994 | |

| BREEDER | AQHA ID NUMBER | CITY | STATE |
|---|---|---|---|
| KADASH KATHY | 1021312 | MONUMENT | COLORADO |

| OWNER | AQHA ID NUMBER | CITY | STATE |
|---|---|---|---|
| KADASH KATHY | 1021312 | MONUMENT | COLORADO |

|  |  |  |  |
|---|---|---|---|
| SIRE | POCO STRIPE | POCO BUENO 0221870 | 0003044 |
| POCO BUENO STRIPE 2345331 | | LADY BEAVER 10 | 0047722 |
| | MISS POCO QUEENIE | POCO PAT 1304300 | 0048570 |
| | | MISS VALU | 0186511 |
| DAM | KING POCO KANDOO | ENTERPRISING KING 1491517 | 0668828 |
| POCO MISS SMOKY 2171815 | | MISS POCO KANDEE | 0948497 |
| | PETE'S SANDY | TOY PETE 0474525 | 0085548 |
| | | BONITA PRIMERA | 0237129 |

MARKINGS

STAR AND SNIP. LEFT HIND SOCK. NO OTHER MARKINGS.

This is to certify that the above named and described horse has been registered in the Stud Book of The American Quarter Horse Association.

PROSPECTIVE PURCHASER — Check the horse's markings, color and age, against this certificate. This certificate is issued in sole reliance on written application submitted by the owner at time of foaling, without further verification by the Association. Ownership of this certificate is retained by the Association, and issued upon express condition that the Association has the continuing privilege to demand immediate return thereof for correction, cancellation, or any other official reason under Association rules, and pending resolution of the matter, the Association may retain possession thereof.

DATE ISSUED

OCTOBER 13, 1994

EXECUTIVE VICE-PRESIDENT

### TRANSFER RECORD

The last name entered hereunder is the present owner of this horse as shown on the records of The American Quarter Horse Association. To transfer the within described horse, make transfer on a separate transfer form or bill of sale, which will be furnished free by the ASSOCIATION. Send it to the office of the American Quarter Horse Association—along with the registration certificate and the transfer fee. The transfer of ownership will then be made on this certificate and mailed as instructed.

| FOR OFFICE USE ONLY - DO NOT WRITE ON THIS CERTIFICATE | | |
|---|---|---|
| Date of Purchase | Name and Address of Owner as Shown by Transfer Record | Attest of Record by Executive Vice-President |
| | | |
| | | |
| | | |
| | | |
| | | |
| | | |

Copyright 1974, AMERICAN QUARTER HORSE ASSOCIATION

may be required before you haul your new horse home to the boarding stable. In some states, a brand inspection by a representative of the state's livestock or animal health department may be necessary when ownership of a horse is transferred.

Again, the buyer must beware. All too often a buyer is told a horse is registered, "but my uncle has the certificate. I'll mail it to you." That horse is considered a grade horse until or unless you receive the registration certificate and a signed transfer from the last owner of record.

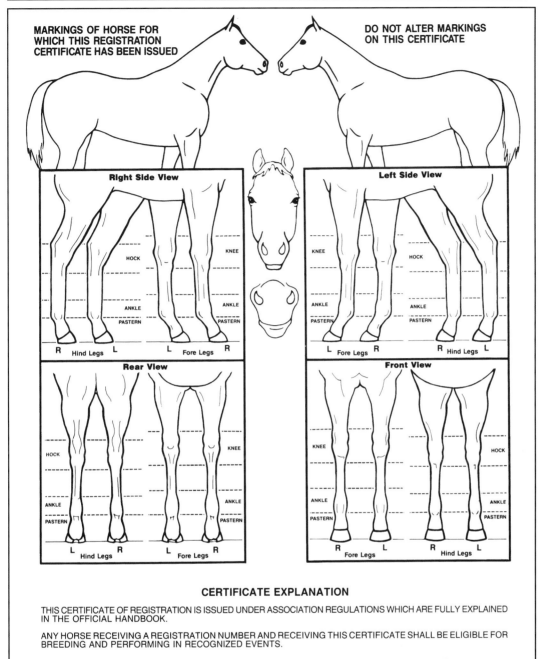

**MARKINGS OF HORSE FOR WHICH THIS REGISTRATION CERTIFICATE HAS BEEN ISSUED**

**DO NOT ALTER MARKINGS ON THIS CERTIFICATE**

Right Side View

Left Side View

HOCK — KNEE — KNEE — HOCK

ANKLE — ANKLE — ANKLE — ANKLE

PASTERN — PASTERN — PASTERN — PASTERN

R Hind Legs L — L Fore Legs R — L Fore Legs R — R Hind Legs L

Rear View

Front View

HOCK — KNEE — KNEE — HOCK

ANKLE — ANKLE — ANKLE — ANKLE

PASTERN — PASTERN — PASTERN — PASTERN

L Hind Legs R — L Fore Legs R — R Fore Legs L — R Hind Legs L

**CERTIFICATE EXPLANATION**

THIS CERTIFICATE OF REGISTRATION IS ISSUED UNDER ASSOCIATION REGULATIONS WHICH ARE FULLY EXPLAINED IN THE OFFICIAL HANDBOOK.

ANY HORSE RECEIVING A REGISTRATION NUMBER AND RECEIVING THIS CERTIFICATE SHALL BE ELIGIBLE FOR BREEDING AND PERFORMING IN RECOGNIZED EVENTS.

**AMERICAN QUARTER HORSE ASSOCIATION**
Amarillo, Texas 79168

When you purchase a registered horse, check to see that the physical description of the horse on the certificate matches the horse you are purchasing. Check the last owner of record on the papers; only he or she can transfer ownership of the horse to you, and a transfer fee usually is required. If the last owner of record is not the person from whom you are buying the horse, you should delay the transaction until the certificate is updated. If you have questions, call the association with which the horse is registered.

# WHAT YOU'RE WILLING TO PAY

## 5

HORSEBACK riding, like most hobbies, costs money. There's no way around it. But all too often, people don't understand that the price of a horse is often the cheapest part of owning one. They don't realize how much it's going to cost to take proper care of the horse, particularly veterinary expenses.

Be realistic. Recognize there is a capital outlay for the horse, and possibly for a barn, truck, or trailer. The expense of maintaining a horse is an ongoing one. Gear must be replaced, veterinarians and farriers have to be paid, and feed and hay must be purchased.

## Cost of the Horse

Establishing the initial investment required to buy a first horse is difficult.

Horse prices vary from one part of the country to another. One breed may be considered a higher-dollar animal than another, in some respects, depending on the location and/or the particular type riding most popular there. Prices can vary greatly within one breed as well, depending on a horse's bloodlines, age, training, show record, or track record.

When the horse market cycles down, the number of mares being bred drops, which later results in fewer available horses to ride. This usually results in higher prices for well-broke mounts, and eventually in more horses being bred once again. Such a cycle affects grade horses as well as registered ones.

If you have been shopping around for a first horse to buy, you probably are familiar with the market in your locale. If you're just

*Purchasing a horse for show usually requires a larger initial investment than does purchasing one for pleasure riding at home.*

beginning to shop, the best horseman you know can help you estimate a purchase-price range, and as you consider prospects, you'll get a better idea of the cost.

Recognize, too, that the price range for a horse strictly suitable for weekend riding shouldn't be as high as the range for a horse capable of winning area pleasure classes or jackpot roping events. A horse competitive in an equine sport at the state or national level will be priced higher accordingly. If you can afford to purchase a state or national champion to ride only on Sunday afternoons, that's great. If not, pay attention to your local market.

The American Horse Council's *Horse Industry Handbook* states that, due to the many factors affecting the cost of a horse, "For determining minimum investment requirements, we have more or less arbitrarily chosen the $800 horse," which is described as "the basic model, non-registered, saddle-trained horse."

Don't lock in on that amount; that's only a starting place to establish the initial investment required to purchase a horse. The horse you want may be lower in price, but more likely will be higher. Knowing the type horse you want to purchase and being familiar with the market in your area are important to feeling comfortable about the price you pay for a first horse.

This cannot be emphasized too much: Let the buyer beware. It's up to you to purchase wisely. Although he can help you avoid some pitfalls, it is not the responsibility of your horseman friend to decide the amount you write on a check, and it's certainly not the seller's.

But suppose you fall in love with a prospect who costs more money than you anticipated spending. You ease your conscience by viewing the purchase as a business investment. You'll keep the horse until the market is up, and then sell him and purchase an even better mount. Or, if the horse is a mare, you'll breed her and sell her foals for top money. Don't kid yourself.

To many first-time horse owners, selling the animal a few years later doesn't seem a big deal—at first. Down the road, selling that first horse could be somewhat akin to selling a good friend.

Breeding a first horse, later on, is a fine idea, but emotions get involved once again. Will you be able to part with the *child* of your first horse? As for selling a foal for top money, it is possible. But it's

likely only if the mare has established quite a reputation on the track or in the show arena, and both pursuits require major investments of time and money.

For most people, that first horse becomes a buddy who shares their hobby; the expense of his companionship is the cost of entertainment.

In any case, there are other considerations. Through accident or injury, a first horse could become unfit to ride, or that first mare might not be easy to settle, or get in foal. Worst of all, horses do die. It's unpleasant to consider, but part of horse ownership is accepting that fact.

# Gear

As for the gear and equipment you need to ride your new horse, Cost and Responsibilities of Ownership in the *Horse Industry Handbook* offers estimates for the basic necessities—saddle, pad, bridle, halter, lead, curry comb, brush, hoof pick, buckets, and blanket. Some of the items, such as the blanket for extreme weather or the saddle, can be purchased used, rather than new. According to the handbook, used saddles can usually be found at about 60 percent of the new price. In other words, a saddle worth about $1,000 new will likely sell for about $600 used.

| Tack and Equipment | Your Estimates |
|---|---|
| Saddle (used). . . . . . . $600 | _____ |
| Bridle. . . . . . . . . . . . .   60 | _____ |
| Pad . . . . . . . . . . . . .   30 | _____ |
| Halter . . . . . . . . . . .   20 | _____ |
| Lead. . . . . . . . . . . . .    8 | _____ |
| Curry comb. . . . . . . .    4 | _____ |
| Hoof pick. . . . . . . . . .    1 | _____ |
| Brush . . . . . . . . . . . .    5 | _____ |
| Buckets . . . . . . . . . . .   35 | _____ |
| Blanket . . . . . . . . . . .   80 | _____ |
| **Total** . . . . . . . . . . . . $843 | _____ |

Here's a look at some of the basic costs of caring for a horse on a daily, monthly, and annual basis. The formula for arriving at a cost has been included so that you can figure, more accurately, the costs based on your local prices for hay, shoeing, and such. See other chapters for more in-depth information on feeding and rations, hoof care, and horse health care.

---

### Forage Costs Per Day

*Cost per bale ÷ 60 (average pounds per bale) = cost per pound of forage.*

_____ ÷ 60 (average pounds per bale) = _____

*Forage cost per pound × pounds fed per day = forage cost per day.*

_____ × _____ = _____

### Grain Costs Per Day

*Cost per bag ÷ 50 (pounds per bag) = cost per pound of grain.*

_____ ÷ 50 (pounds per bag) = _____

*Grain cost per pound × pounds fed per day = grain cost per day.*

_____ × _____ = _____

### Daily Feed Expense

*Forage cost + grain cost + salt and mineral cost = daily expense.*

_____ + _____ + _____ = _____

---

# Boarding

If you board your horse, the cost for your facilities is an outright expense, usually payable on a monthly basis. Boarding costs can range from $50 a month for no-frills pasture care up to $400 a month for full care in a stall.

# Self-Care

Feed costs vary greatly from place to place because of differing soil types and weather conditions. For prices of hay and grain in your area, call your local feed stores to determine average prices.

The broadest of guidelines are used in the example for figuring feed costs for a

---

### Hoof Care Expense

*Cost per farrier call × number of visits per year = hoof care expense per year.*

_____ × _____ = _____

*Annual hoof care expense ÷ 12 = average monthly hoof care expense.*

_____ ÷ 12 = _____

---

1,000-pound mature horse undergoing light work, which is considered 1 to 3 hours of work daily. In this example, it is assumed there is no pasture forage available, so a full ration of hay and grain must be considered when figuring feed costs.

A thumb rule for a horse's daily ration suggests $1\frac{1}{4}$-$1\frac{1}{2}$ pounds of forage and $\frac{1}{3}$-$\frac{1}{2}$ pound of grain per 100 pounds of body weight. To simplify the mathematics, let's use $1\frac{1}{2}$ pounds of forage and $\frac{1}{2}$ pound of grain. That translates into 15 pounds of forage (1,000/100 = 10 x $1\frac{1}{2}$ pounds) and 5 pounds of grain daily (10 x $\frac{1}{2}$ pound).

Let's assume that a 60-pound bale of hay costs $5. That translates into $8\frac{1}{3}$ cents per pound. Multiply that by 15 pounds, and you get $1.25. That's the daily cost of hay.

Daily grain expense is figured the same way. Oats and mixed feeds are usually sacked in 50-pound bags, so the cost per bag of grain divided by 50 yields a cost per pound of grain. The cost per pound is multiplied by 5, the pounds of grain in the sample daily ration, to determine the daily grain expense.

Use the work sheet shown to estimate feed costs in your area.

Remember, too, that horses need salt and minerals available, in addition to feed. Although the cost of a small salt or mineral brick seems negligible, it can add up. The *Horse Industry Handbook* uses 10 cents per day per horse.

# Shoeing and Trimming

Even if you are not riding your horse year-round, his feet must be trimmed regularly, about every 6-8 weeks. This is a minimum of six times per year, and it can be as many as nine or more times. Shoeing costs more than trimming.

To estimate hoof care costs, multiply the cost of trimming your horse by six. Also multiply the cost by nine. The two resulting amounts will give a range to use in estimating expenses for trimming.

If you plan to shoe year-round, substitute the cost of shoeing for that of trimming. Should your riding plans require shoeing for only about 6 months each year, figure the costs accordingly, with half the cost figured on trimming and the other half based on shoeing. Again, contact about three sources in your area to determine the going rates for trimming and/or shoeing.

## Veterinary Costs

For veterinary care, the *Horse Industry Handbook* offers $.50 per day as a guideline, with no explanation of the costs included. Many health care costs will be paid directly to the veterinarian—getting a Coggins test, for example. Your state's livestock health regulations will affect the frequency of testing, which is usually every 6 or 12 months.

Also consult with your veterinarian about a good program to control internal parasites. Deworming, however, has been simplified with the paste medications and products that can be mixed with feed. Many horsemen figure only the cost of the dewormer into the budget and, about every 2 months, deworm the horses themselves. Multiply the cost per application times six, which reflects the 2-month deworming schedule, to get an annual cost for deworming per head.

Vaccinations vary with your location. But the standard ones are tetanus, influenza, strangles, equine encephalomyelitis, and rhinopneumonitis. Ask the veterinarian how often your horse should be immunized during the coming year and for an estimated cost for each vaccination, along with any boosters. Total the cost of the recommended vaccinations and divide that amount by 12 to arrive at an average cost per month.

## Parts and Labor

Bear in mind, this short form does not include labor costs, should you hire someone to help you feed or clean stalls. No cost is shown for the replacement of tack or for tack repair; nor is any out-of-pocket repair cost included for the facilities. Fences, stalls, water lines, and such eventually require repair, and buckets, hoses, and feeders must be replaced occasionally. Should you plan on weekly lessons with an instructor or sending your horse to a trainer, those are additional expenses to consider.

Horse ownership is costly, but many people consider the money well-spent since riding opens the door to many new experiences.

---

### Health Care Expense

Coggins tests . . . . . . $_____
Deworming . . . . . . . _____
Vaccinations . . . . . . _____

**Total annual cost**  $_____

Total annual cost ÷ 12 = *monthly heath care cost.*

_____ ÷ 12 = _____

---

### Summary of Horse Care Costs

| Item | cost/day | cost/month | cost/year |
|---|---|---|---|
| Feed expense . . . . . . . . $_____ | | _____ | _____ |
| Hoof care expense . . . . _____ | | _____ | _____ |
| Health care expense. . . _____ | | _____ | _____ |
| **Total out-of-pocket**  $_____ | | _____ | _____ |

# WHERE TO KEEP YOUR HORSE

**6**

ONCE YOU have decided to buy a horse, likely the next and most pressing problem is deciding where to keep your horse. As the horse developed through the ages, certain characteristics became inherent in his makeup. These characteristics, to an extent, have some bearing on what a horse today needs in his environment to be comfortable and content. As a horse owner, you will use manmade facilities to meet the horse's needs that were once supplied by his natural environment.

In earlier times, horses banded together in herds and roamed the land. Herbivorous animals, they were constantly on the move in search of good grazing, continuously eating small amounts during a day's time. Being a herd animal means that a horse is a social creature who likes the company of his own kind. The leisurely grazing habit is still with him. The horse's digestive system is somewhat small for his size, better suited to several smaller meals rather than a few large ones. The horse lived in the great outdoors, relying on his heavier winter haircoat and learning to make the most of nature's provisions for protection from the elements.

The horse today is not much different from his predecessors. A little space to wander suits his nature, and a simple shelter is adequate to approximate the protection nature once provided. Of course, the more room you can provide your horse to wander and to graze, the better, but most people don't have acres of

*Boarding a horse in pasture is inexpensive, but makes it difficult to catch the horse. He's also more likely to be injured if he and his pasture mates don't get along.*

pasture land. Land costs and zoning restrictions are prohibitive in many cases.

Most horse owners do the best they can with what is available to provide adequate facilities for their horses. What's available may be a few well-fenced acres and a loafing shed, that you either own or rent, or a stall with a run or turnout paddock at the local boarding stable. Whether you plan to board your horse or keep him at home, certain necessities common to both situations must be considered. The amenities, more often for the rider's benefit than for the horse's, are sometimes time- and/or labor-saving, or just plain fun. All of it has a price.

Since first-time horse owners often board their horses elsewhere, the following focuses on horse facilities from that perspective. However, the same considerations apply to the horse owner with his own facilities. If you are fortunate enough to own land for horses, *Western Horseman's* book *Roofs and Rails* offers information about designing, planning, and building your own barn, stalls, and fences.

# Types of Board

If boarding a horse is your only practical option, there are three types: stable, corral, and pasture board.

When stable boarding a horse, you pay to keep your horse inside a stable. In some cases, the stall may have an attached run so your horse can go outdoors or in, as he prefers. In other cases, the outfit may provide turnout paddocks or pens for your use, with the horse confined to his stall until he is taken from it and turned loose.

When you pay stable board, or stall board, as it's sometimes known, you pay full board or partial board. Full board means the provider takes care of everything from feeding and watering to stall cleaning. Partial board arrangements vary, with a horse owner purchasing his own feed, for example, or cleaning his horse's

*Individual runs allow the mares and foals in this facility room to move around.*

stall, rather than paying for those things.

Corral boarding means your horse is kept in a small corral or pen, with some type of inexpensive shelter. This type of boarding is cheaper than stall boarding.

Pasture board typically means you pay to keep your horse in a pasture. Your horse may have his own pasture, but usually several horses are run together in one pasture. A few trees in the pasture can provide a windbreak and shade from the sun, as can a loafing shed.

A loafing shed is a simple, three-sided, covered structure that may have a feeder of some sort and a water supply nearby. Such a shed can provide adequate shade, a windbreak, and protection from rain and snow for your horse. An enclosed feed and/or tack room is often built on one end of the shed for the horseman's convenience.

It is important that the loafing shed has ample room for the number of head running together in a pasture. As herd animals, horses establish a distinct social order among members of their group, with the more dominant animals nipping or kicking to put those lower in the pecking order in their proper place. A loafing shed should offer sufficient room for this kind of horseplay, allowing a horse room to dodge, or even leave the shed if necessary, without being trapped by a more dominant animal.

## Evaluating a Facility

There are several considerations when selecting a boarding facility. Among the first is finding out how many horses are boarded there. A large number of boarders is fine if you prefer lots of company when you're at the barn. But many boarders may not be so great if the stable doesn't have the necessary help to provide good care of the horses and to take proper care of the facility. When you visit a facility, talk to some of the boarders, if possible, and ask what they like or dislike about the facility.

Some stables specialize in catering to horsemen pursuing a certain aspect of riding—dressage, for example. Another outfit might have access to any number of riding trails and draw primarily pleasure

and trail riders. A telephone call to the stables can answer some of your questions, but a visit is required to answer others.

Primary among them, how do the horses boarded there look? Do they appear healthy, in good flesh with shiny haircoats? Or do the horses seem lethargic, with dull coats and the tail hair rubbed out? This could be an indication of a parasite problem. Do the barns and stalls appear neat and clean? Are the fences safe? The facilities need not be fancy, but should be serviceable. If what you find when you visit a boarding stable is pleasing, it's time to find out more about the necessities and the amenities offered there, along with the costs, and take a closer look at the operation.

Check the necessities first—the physical facilities. Whether you select stable board with a run or turnout paddock, or pasture board, take a close look at your horse's potential home. As you walk into the barn, consider the aisleway. Is it clean with good footing? Is it wide enough to allow two horses to meet and safely pass one another? Or is the aisle full of potential problems— an unsecured feed supply, a roll of wire, or junk items piled high—where one misstep could yield disastrous results?

## Stalls

Look at the stall door. Is the latch one that's relatively horse-proof, so that a bored animal entertaining himself won't be so likely to turn himself out? Open the stall door. If the latch is a sliding one, does the end retract far enough that it won't poke an unsuspecting horse in the side when he is led out the door? A hinged door often sags, unless it is well-maintained, and can create an obstruction in the aisleway when it is opened. Better yet is a sliding door that moves flush against the front wall of the stall. Is the door opening itself at least 4 feet wide?

Consider the size of the stall. The minimum size is 10 feet by 10 feet, 10 by 12 is better, and 12 by 12 or larger gives the horse even more comfort. There should be a minimum of 8 feet of clearance overhead in the stall area.

Look at the interior walls. They should be flush with the floor so that a horse can't

*Here's a well-built stall that provides for a horse's safety and at the same time allows him to see what's going on around the barn. It is advisable, however, to take the halter off any horse before putting him back in the stall or out to pasture. Leaving halters on horses is dangerous.*

get a foot caught where the floor and wall join. For a large animal, the horse has relatively small feet, and a 4- or 5-inch opening is a potential trap. Ideally, stall walls should be solid and sturdily built; a stalled horse may kick at a fly or at the neighboring horse and hit the wall, which should be substantial enough to withstand the blow.

Some stall partitions are solid almost to the ceiling, leaving a space for ventilation above. Often the solid portion extends to about 5 feet, with the upper portion having bars or screens. Since the horse is a social creature and one who is apt to become bored when confined to a stall, bars or screens allow him access to the world around him. He can see other horses, and the barn activity provides diversionary entertainment. If bars or

screens are used, again the spacing should be small enough that a horse can't get caught in it—3 inches or less on bar spacing for a mature horse and about 2 inches square or smaller for mesh wiring. The stall's interior surface should be smooth, with no nails or hardware sticking out to cut or scrape the horse.

Stall flooring and bedding are important considerations, particularly if your horse is confined most of the time. Keeping a stall clean is an ongoing task, and the type flooring and bedding used contribute to the ease or difficulty of the chore. If you are stable boarding where full service is offered, that is likely not so much of concern to you since a stable employee will be doing the cleaning. So check to see if the stalls are clean and well-bedded.

However, if you are responsible for stall cleaning, the flooring and bedding used in your area often depends on what is locally available at the most reasonable cost. In this respect, visiting boarding stables will be an education. You will find out the advantages and disadvantages, as the stable owners see them, of different materials.

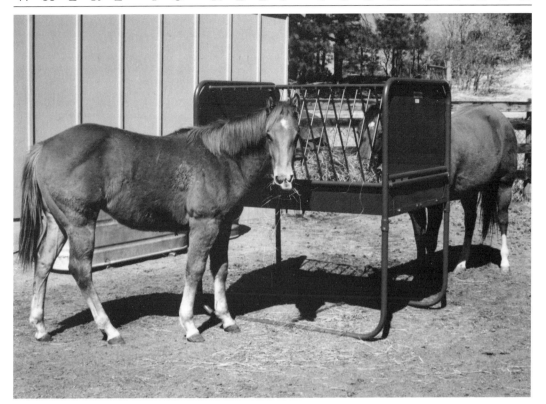

*This free-standing feeder holds both hay in the V-insert at the top and grain in the lower portion. It is sturdy and safe.*

# Feeders and Waterers

Each stall should be equipped with a feeder and a supply of fresh water. There are a variety of feeders on the market today. A feeder can be a simple soft rubber or molded plastic tub placed on the floor of the stall, but a horse sometimes paws with his front feet as he eats, turning the tub over. As a result, he must sift through bedding and waste to get to his grain. The rubber tub can be placed inside an old tire to help prevent this, but that takes valuable floor space in the stall itself.

Feeders are most often attached to the stall walls, where they should be placed high enough that a horse can't get a foot caught in the feeder. If the feeder is a simple wooden box fastened to the wall, the surfaces should be smooth with no exposed nails, nailheads, or splinters.

The hay rack should also be placed high enough to prevent a horse from getting a foot caught. Some hay racks have bars spaced wide enough that a horse might free himself if he gets a foot through the bars. The downside, however, is that the hay often falls through the rack and onto the floor.

A good choice is a combination hay and grain feeder, with the hay rack placed over a grain box. As the horse eats his hay, the smaller stems and leaves fall into the grain box for consumption later. As with any feeder, this type shouldn't be too low to the ground, with the bottom of the feeder $3\frac{1}{2}$ to $4\frac{1}{2}$ feet from the ground.

Depending on the board agreement made between you and the stable, the stables may supply grain and hay and feed your horse daily, or you may purchase feed and perform the daily chores yourself. Either way, notice how the grain and hay are stored. Any stored grains should be well-secured to prevent a horse getting into the supply.

Despite the fact the horse is big and stout, his digestive system is delicate, and

*This water bucket is well-placed in a soundly built stall. The bucket is fastened at the correct height for the young horse, and it's in a sturdy holder.*

an overload of grain can be deadly. Hay should be stacked nearby, but with an eye toward fire prevention. In addition, fresh hay too tightly stacked in an unventilated area gives rise to mold, which can cause stomach problems for the horse. Check the hay being fed by the stable. Good hay is green, smells good, and is free of dust, weeds, and mold.

The water supply at any barn is of utmost importance. A hydrant, hose, and bucket can suffice if used thoughtfully, particularly when your climate is a cold one. Hydrants, usually found in the aisleway, should be positioned so that they don't inadvertently get wrecked when a manure-spreader or tractor comes down the aisleway. The hose should be sturdy; it will likely get stepped on from time to time. During cold weather, it may be necessary to drain hoses to prevent freezing and splitting.

If employees at the boarding stable routinely water horses several times a day, one large bucket in the stall should suffice. Better yet is having two buckets, each holding several gallons, to ensure your horse has an ample supply between routine refills. The buckets should be emptied daily, then refilled, and washed out periodically. As with feeders, water buckets should be hung high enough so that a horse can't get a foot caught.

Another consideration is how a water bucket is attached to the stall wall. Hanging the bail of the bucket over a hook attached to the barn wall is easy for the person watering. But a horse who is startled while drinking is apt to tear a nostril on the hook. An eye bolt on the wall is better, with a double-ended snap fastened to it and to the bucket.

In colder climates, a tank-heater is a good investment. Horses require a volume of water daily and are less apt to drink a sufficient amount if the water is extremely cold. Heaters suitable for buckets or larger troughs are commercially available.

Some boarding stables have automatic waterers installed for convenience. These should be checked daily to ensure that they are working. As with feeders and water buckets, an automatic waterer should be installed with the horse's safety in mind, with nothing in the design that could trap an animal's leg.

## Lighting, Ventilation, and Manure Disposal

Lighting in the barn is another consideration. The use of skylights brightens a barn in general, and often each stall has a window opening in the outside wall, which helps in ventilation as well. If there are lights in the aisleway or anywhere in the stall that a horse can reach, be sure the bulb has a protective covering. Check, too, that electric wiring is enclosed in conduits so a horse (or rodents) can't chew it.

Good barn ventilation ensures that the horse doesn't get overwhelmed by the ammonia smell of urine. Take a good whiff of air when you walk into a barn. Does it smell just of horse and hay, or is the odor heavy and rank? If so, you have

*This fencing is both safe and suitable for a mature horse.*

an idea about the air flow through the barn and/or the stall-cleaning habits of the people there.

Stall cleaning leads to the problem of manure disposal. Whether the barn is your own or someone else's, the problem must be dealt with. How it is resolved sometimes depends on the type bedding used in stalls, as well as local ordinances or restrictions. Often manure goes into a compost heap for future use, is put into a manure spreader for later use as pasture fertilizer, or is put into a commercial dumpster.

## Pasture, Loafing Shed, and Fencing

If your horse is going to live in a pasture with a loafing shed, study the structure, along with the feeding and watering equipment in the same way you would consider a stall in a barn. Look for smooth edges in the building itself, and be sure any nails and hardware are properly fastened down. Look for potential booby traps for a horse around the feed and water troughs.

Fencing is a primary consideration when pasturing a horse. Check for broken boards with jagged edges if the fence is a wooden one. The spacing of the rails should be wide enough that a horse's foot can't get caught, but small enough that the horse won't be tempted to put his head and neck between them.

If wire mesh is used for fencing, be sure the mesh is small enough that a horse's foot won't go through it. This type fencing usually extends to the ground, so check to see that your horse can't wedge a foot between the fence and the ground.

Barbed-wire fencing is not suitable for horses, period. It is too dangerous. Pipe makes good fencing. Nowadays, PVC and other modern high-tech materials are often used as well. Corral fencing should be at least 6 feet, and pasture fencing about 5 feet high. Don't be surprised to find electric fencing around a horse pasture, even at the top of a board fence. A

*Because horses love to rub, fencing needs to be stout and safe.*

hot-wire, as it's called, gives a horse a healthy respect for any barrier. This often prevents a horse from leaning over or on the fence, which can result in broken boards, wire pulled away from fence posts, and less stability in the support posts.

Check the fence's corner posts and line posts for decay. If steel T-posts have been used to support the fence, the blades at the base should be well into the ground. Also, plastic safety caps should be on top of steel posts to prevent a horse from cutting or impaling himself on them. Line posts should be properly spaced to help prevent sagging in whatever type fencing material is used.

Look at pasture gates in much the same way you would a stall door. Is the gate of sufficient width and height? Does it fit the opening well without gaps that could trap a horse? If it's aluminum, are the metal edges rounded? Does the gate fasten securely? On light aluminum gates, notice if the hinges are dropped down onto upright supports. In this instance, horses have been known to bump the gate, lifting the gate from the supports. The gate falls partially over, and the resulting gap tempts the horse, who tries to walk through and becomes entangled. A couple of lengths of chain and snaps, attached to the support post at the top and bottom of the gate, can help prevent a potential wreck in this case.

## Amenities

By now you're getting an idea of the type facilities that can safely contain your horse. When a boarding stable offers amenities such as round pens, arenas, runs, and turnout paddocks, check them in much the same manner, with an eye to the horse's safety.

Often portable metal panels are used for stall runs or round pens. Again, check for rough edges and secure fastenings between the panels and around the gates.

*Weigh the amenities at each facility. It may be worth it to you to have access to a round pen or an arena.*

The more uneven the ground the panels are on, the more important it is to check where the panels attach to one another. If it looks like a good bump could shake one panel loose from another, tie the panels together, just to be on the safe side.

Other amenities at horse barns include wash racks or well-drained areas with a handy water supply, sometimes including both hot and cold water. Tack storage is often provided for the convenience of boarders at a stable. And, if you own a horse trailer, it can serve as a storage area as well. Some stables have sufficient room to provide permanent trailer parking for their boarders. Public boarding facilities often offer riding lessons or have trainers on the premises. In addition, activities such as playdays or trail rides are sometimes scheduled for the boarders.

Even though your first horse is a new-found companion, boarding him involves taking care of business. Ask the stable manager what specifically is included in the cost of a month's board—feed and feeding, stall-cleaning, daily turnout, and such. What is the barn's policy regarding emergency veterinary care? Does a farrier come

to the barn regularly, or is hoof care solely your responsibility? Does the stable have rules applying to all boarders? Does the stable require a written board agreement?

Questions of liability can arise in such a situation. Several states in recent years have enacted equine liability statutes that do give stable owners some protection, so it is to your advantage to find out who's responsible and for what in your area.

Although many people dislike approaching their sport and hobby in such a businesslike manner, such agreements often help eliminate misunderstandings. Above all, remember that other boarders and stable employees would like to receive the same courtesy and consideration you wish for yourself.

# WHERE TO RIDE YOUR HORSE

**7**

WHEN CONSIDERING where to keep your horse, also take into consideration where you can ride your horse. Whether you board your horse or use your own facilities, there is likely some space around the barn area available for riding. It may be only a round pen and arena, or a few acres of pasture, so take a look around the neighborhood to see if riding out from the barn is feasible as well.

Perhaps the stable where you board your horse or the neighborhood in which you live has riding trails provided. In recent years, some areas zoned for horses have been developed with such trails writ-ten into neighborhood planning. If that's the case, you are sure to have fellow horse-men close by. Covenants and restrictions, however, may limit your riding to certain, specific areas.

Local, state, and national park and forest areas sometimes have trails open for horse traffic, although recreational areas within such parks—picnic, campsite, and swimming areas—may not be. Sometimes riding the trails is acceptable, but indis-criminately tying your horse to a tree may not be, depending on the park's environ-mental policies. Don't assume you can ride your horse there. Ask people in the

*Some horsemen enjoy riding vacations and get-ting a closer look at vari-ous parts of the country.*

area, or call the recreational area's headquarters and find out what is permissible. In the past few years, horse traffic has been curtailed in many park areas, so it's wise to check the rules.

You might consider joining a club of trail riding enthusiasts in your area, if that's how you plan to enjoy your horse. Organized clubs sometimes gain access to areas for riding, even privately owned land, that may not be open to the individual. This is especially true if the club has a good track record for honoring any agreements about trash cleanup and such that have been made in the past. Too, such clubs often sponsor regular day or weekend rides on a monthly basis.

If you are pursuing your riding hobby in the competitive arena, most areas have riding clubs to join. Membership sometimes includes a gate key to the premises and/or the arena, that can be used at the member's convenience. There is usually ample parking for trailers, and sometimes stalls are available as well. Such clubs often plan playdays and horse shows for their members and often sponsor area 4-H riding projects for young people.

In addition, a club sometimes rents its facilities to a group of horsemen interested in a particular sport—team roping, for example—for practice or to hold a competition. Either way, club members are given a firsthand opportunity to see other aspects of riding.

No matter where you choose to ride, however, always put safety first. Look at what is underfoot. Not only is the trash your horse steps over a consideration, the footing he steps on is important. Dirt trails and arenas are great for riding, and nothing is more enticing than acres of pasture land, but the latter can be full of gopher holes and such. Too, lush green grass can be slick underfoot, and thorns or cactus can make things unpleasant for your horse.

Riding regularly on gravel and rock is not recommended. Pavement of any sort can cause problems for the horse and rider; the slick surface makes holding your footing at any speed difficult. Riding on hard, slick surfaces is inviting a fall, particularly with a shod horse or a fast-moving one.

Look overhead as well as underfoot

**Again, riding a well-broke horse, along with practicing common courtesy, can prevent problems.**

57

*State parks and national forests sometimes have equestrian trails within their boundaries.*

when you ride. Many forest trails were designed and cleared with hikers in mind, not for the additional height of a rider on horseback. Overhanging limbs can be a problem not only for the rider, but also for the person riding behind him; the back-lash, when a tree limb is held back and then turned loose, can be substantial. Clothes lines, support wires for power poles, and the edges of low shed roofs can be tough on the rider who isn't paying attention to where he's going.

Having a broke horse, as previously described, is a real boon when approaching obstacles on the trail or at the saddle club grounds. Approaching an obstacle may involve stepping your horse over a downed tree or a pile of cross-ties, opening a gate from horseback, wading through a sizable mud hole, negotiating between parked trailers, taking your coat from the fence or the mail from the box, or simply passing by a trash bag or barrel. The more broke your horse is, the more readily he will take such situations in stride.

No one particularly wants to ride horseback alongside a roadway, but in more populous areas, this may be one of a very few options. Too, riding alongside the road may be the only way you can get to another, more desirable place to ride, such as a friend's pasture, a public riding trail, or park area. If you can avoid riding horseback around traffic, you are far wiser to do so. Under no circumstances should children without adult supervision ride in this manner.

If you must ride alongside a roadway, make safety your major consideration. Here is where having a broke horse, as described earlier, becomes important; a well-seasoned, broke horse can better handle the noise and motion of fast-moving vehicles.

Check the traffic on any road before you venture out with your horse. A large volume of traffic whizzing by can be unsettling to both you and your animal, even though the traffic isn't a surprise and you both know to expect it.

Many roadways have wide shoulders

58

*Riding alongside a road is never desirable but may be necessary in some circumstances.*

or rights-of-way. If more than one person is riding and space allows, the more experienced rider and horse might travel between the less experienced pair and the roadway. This provides a buffer zone for the novice. Riding immediately adjacent to a road or on it is not a good idea.

If you do ride alongside the road, check the ground frequently for strands of wire, cans, and broken bottles; all are potential problems. Having a horse cut or injured when walking over roadside trash is not uncommon. Too, blowing trash along the roadside can startle a horse, possibly causing him to shy into the road and into the path of a vehicle.

The more you ride, the more likely you'll be around other people riding. Your plans call for reasonable control of yourself and your horse to keep the two of you out of trouble. Other people, however, may not have the same control of their horses, their dogs, and even their children. Again, riding a well-broke horse, along with practicing common

courtesy, can prevent problems.

At first, remembering all the things to consider, when you ride away from the barn, may seem troublesome. However, after a few rides, periodically checking underfoot and overhead will become second nature to you, as will negotiating more common obstacles. Don't get in such a hurry, when riding your new horse, that you fail to make safety your prime consideration. It shows good horsemanship on your part and helps you make the most of what your new mount has to offer you.

# THE GEAR YOU NEED

**8**

WHEN YOU purchase your horse, you'll need the appropriate gear and equipment. Many choices are available for almost any piece of tack you need, and many items can be purchased used, rather than new. It's all a bit overwhelming to the newcomer in the horse industry.

Appearance is important in that a saddle must be appealing enough to warrant purchasing. And the better the quality of the leather used and the stitching that holds it together, the longer a saddle will be of service. However, it's what's underneath a saddle that really counts.

But the most important factor to consider is fit—for both the horse and rider. In recent

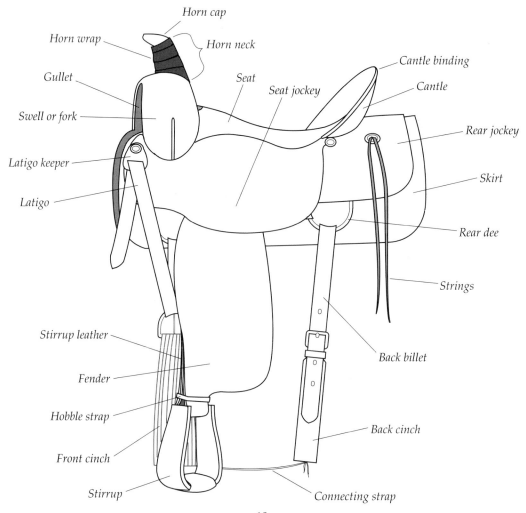

*The parts of the saddle.*

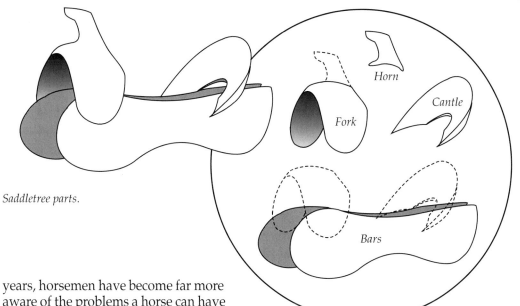

*Saddletree parts.*

Horn

Fork

Cantle

Bars

*A-fork or slick-fork.*

years, horsemen have become far more aware of the problems a horse can have that can be caused by an ill-fitting saddle—jigging, short strides, or an unhappy attitude, plus a sore back and withers.

So get help in selecting the best fitting saddle. Try to understand why saddle fit is important to you and to the horse. Riding a new horse is challenge enough without him dancing around because he is being pinched by a poorly fitted saddle. Nor can you give horsemanship your best effort if your saddle doesn't fit you properly or is uncomfortable.

Your preferences in tack selection will probably change over time. For many people starting to ride, a saddle not too extreme in any aspect of its design works well. Primary consideration should be given to safety in the design and strength in the construction. Be a wise consumer. Know what parts of a saddle are subject to the most stress before you make a purchase. In this case, knowledge contributes to your riding safety.

# Parts of a Saddle

**Tree:** The foundation or frame around which a saddle is built. In most trees, separate parts made of wood—the horn, fork, cantle, and bars—are laminated together, then covered with rawhide for additional strength. In recent years, saddlemakers have made trees of fiberglass, Ralide®, and other materials, but the wooden tree is still the standard in the industry.

A tree, or a saddle, is often described by the use for which it is intended. A roping saddle, for example, has a horn suitable for dallying and a lower cantle and wide

stirrups to facilitate a quick dismount. Some tree designs have been named for the individuals or companies who first made them. A committee of a rodeo association approved the association or committee tree for use in a specific event.

**Bars:** They should fit smoothly along the length of the horse's back and evenly distribute the pressure and weight of the rider and saddle. With a good fit, a saddle is less likely to sore the back. Both the length and the angle of the bars affect how comfortably a saddle fits a horse.

**Fork:** Fork design gives shape and definition to the front of a saddle. An A-fork is just what its name implies; the front of the saddle looks like an A as it rises from the bars to the horn. Other fork styles are somewhat broader in appearance, with more swell to the fork. The more swell to a fork, the more support you feel, for example, when riding downhill.

**Gullet:** The design of the fork, as well as the angle of the bars, helps determine the width and height of the saddle gullet. This, in turn, affects how well a saddletree fits a horse's withers.

The saddle must clear a horse's withers. Too low a fit here and a horse can become

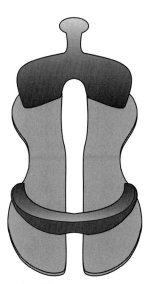

*Swell-fork.*

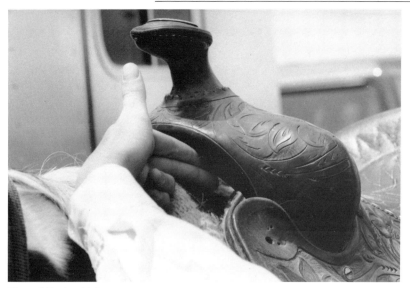

*The saddle should fit over the withers with room to spare.*

support in a higher position on the rider's back. A low cantle is better, however, for quick dismounts.

**Seat:** If the bars determine how comfortable a saddle is on a horse's back, the seat design is equally important to the rider's comfort. Saddle seats are sized in inches and measured from the base of the horn, lengthwise along the seat, to the center of the cantle, at the top. A youth saddle has a shorter seat—14 inches, for example—than that of a saddle for adults—generally 15 or 16 inches. The size of a person's "seat" and thighs determines the length needed.

Too short a seat, in any case, forces you to ride in a less than satisfactory position. A little extra room in the seat is much better than a seat too short. Your best bet is to test-ride the saddle.

Don't rely on seat measurement alone to determine the best-fitting saddle. The shape of the seat, as it forms to the swells of the fork, affects the fit, too, as does cantle design. With a low cantle and a shorter seat, for example, most people tend to "overflow" the back of the saddle. This puts more weight over a horse's loins, subjecting him to possible soreness. A narrow seat and throat will be more comfortable for women, because their thighs are shaped differently.

**Jockeys:** The front jockeys, seat jockeys, and rear jockeys overlay the rigging and hardware attached underneath. Generally, the smoother and tighter the jockeys are constructed, the fewer lumps and bumps, particularly under your legs.

**Skirts:** These are usually lined with sheepskin, although some synthetic materials can be substituted. Skirts can be round or square, with larger skirts contributing more to overall saddle weight.

**Fender:** With stirrup length properly adjusted, your knee shouldn't extend over a fender's front edge; this could chafe your leg. Fenders for youth saddles are sized proportionately smaller, and sometimes short-legged adults find a youth-sized fender works well for them.

Look under the seat jockey to see if the leather at the top of the fender has been tapered to join the stirrup leather. If not, the fender will feel bulky to you and provide less freedom for movement.

sore quickly. A good rule of thumb: You should be able to comfortably fit two fingers in the gullet of the saddle, between the saddle pad and directly under the horn, without feeling cramped.

Saddles generally measure from 5½ inches across the gullet to 6¾ inches. Again, a middle-of-the-road approach, in this case a saddle with about 6 inches at the gullet, works for many horses. Backs vary so much today within a breed that a saddle described as having a Quarter Horse tree does not necessarily fit all Quarter Horses. The same holds true for Arabian trees and all Arabian horses.

**Horn:** This may be tall or short, thick or thin, or with a large horn cap or a small one. The angle used in attaching a horn to a tree also varies. As with other equipment decisions, your choice of horn is determined somewhat by the use you plan to make of it, whether you plan to hold on to it for cutting or dally on it for team roping.

**Cantle:** The term high-backed saddle or low-backed saddle refers to the cantle design used in a saddletree. A high-backed saddle can seem more snug in fit than a low one, given the same seat measurement, simply because it offers more

The bottom of a fender absorbs much sweat where it hangs along a horse's side. Unless regularly cleaned and conditioned, the leather can become hard and stiff, making the fender uncomfortable.

**Stirrup Leather:** One of the most stressed parts on a saddle, this should be checked regularly for worn or weak areas, for safety's sake. A stirrup leather goes over the bar in a saddletree and attaches to the top of the fender. Most stirrup leathers nowadays use Blevins buckles, which makes adjusting the length an easy and quick process.

**Stirrup:** Generally, stirrups are made of wood, but in recent years synthetics have been used, as well as solid metal. Wooden stirrups often have lightweight metal bound to the sides, and the entire stirrup is wrapped in leather or rawhide, which adds strength. The small leather strap, above the top of the stirrup and around the tapered portion of the fender, is a stirrup hobble and binds the stirrup leather and fender together.

Among the more common stirrup styles are the deep and wide-treaded roper, the bell-bottomed stirrup, or the old-style oxbow. Whatever the style, be sure the stirrup size is appropriate to the size of the rider's feet.

A child's small foot, boot heel and all, could go all the way through an adult-sized stirrup. If the child falls, he could hang up, as it's called, and be dragged, rather than falling cleanly to the ground. An overlarge stirrup creates a high-risk situation for a person of any age, but particularly for a child. On the other hand, some stirrups are not big enough for boots with thick, wide soles or overshoes. This can also result in a person getting hung up and dragged.

Stirrups should hang at a 45-degree angle. If they hang parallel to the horse, they force your lower legs into an awkward and tiring position. The solution: Run an old broomstick or 2 by 4 through both stirrups. Do this whenever you're not using your saddle. The results won't be immediate, but over a period of time, the fenders and stirrup leathers will shape to a more comfortable position.

**Keepers, Carriers, and Strings:** On the near side, a latigo carrier is used to keep

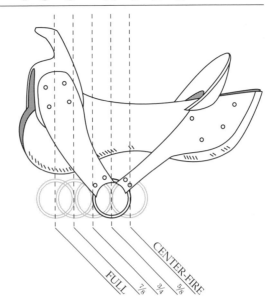

*Rigging positions.*

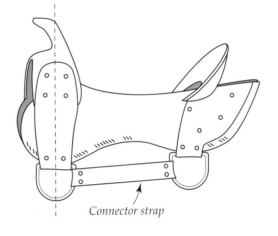

*Double rigging in full position.*

Connector strap

extra latigo from dragging around a horse's legs. On the saddle's far side, a vertically slotted keeper is used to buckle up both front and back cinches so they don't drag on the ground as the saddle is being carried by someone afoot.

Nowadays, some saddles don't have strings at all, or the strings are kept wrapped up short, out of the way. Strings are used to tie on a jacket or slicker, or can be cut off, if necessary, for making minor tack repairs in an emergency.

**Rigging:** Whatever the rigging style, it attaches the cinch that secures the saddle to a horse. Rigging construction is important, even though it's often unseen. The quality of the leather used in rigging a saddle is a primary consideration. If you are considering a used saddle, check the rigging closely for dry-rot. Notice how the

*Three-way rigging plate in-skirt.*

*Skirt*

rigging is attached to a saddle. Wood screws are far more reliable than staples. No matter how eye-appealing the saddle or how good a bargain it is, if the rigging construction isn't strong, you are not riding safely.

The leather in a single- or double-rigged saddle is screwed to the tree. In-skirt rigging uses flat-plate hardware, rather than rings, that is sewn into the saddle skirt. Although less bulky, in-skirt rigging puts greater stress on the skirts and is more difficult to repair.

Brass, bronze, or stainless steel are favored for rigging hardware. Aluminum, for example, leaves gray marks as it rubs against the leather and is considered less durable.

The rigging type and its position on the saddle affect the weight distribution on a horse's back and the amount of bulk under a rider's leg. Rigging positions range from near the front of the saddle (full position) to almost directly under the rider's leg (center-fire). Test-ride as many saddles as possible to discover which suits you best.

**Cinches:** Cinches come in many styles and materials. Mohair cinches have been used for years and don't rot as easily, for example, as cotton ones do. Nylon cinches are popular, but they can gall a horse sometimes. In recent years, wool or synthetic fleece has been used over nylon cinches, but the fleece picks up burrs and such and is hard to keep clean. Leather cinches have met with success as have urethane and neoprene cinches; all are easy to clean and seem comfortable for a horse.

Cinches are sized in even-numbered inches—28, 30, 32, etc. Should you need a replacement, measure from the outside of the ring on one end to the outside ring on the other end of the cinch.

Sweat, combined with the stress placed on a cinch, latigo, or off-billet, makes these prime targets for wear, and regular cleaning is important to minimize deterioration. All three parts should be checked regularly and replaced when necessary to reduce the risk of accident.

A rear cinch helps stabilize a saddle on a horse's back when he is used for roping, for example. For most riding, however, it is not necessary.

**Extras and Eye Appeal:** It's the visible saddle parts that catch your eye when you shop for a saddle—tooling, rawhide trim, silver lacing, cornerplates, and such. Bear in mind that all these aspects of the saddlemaker's art, however eye-appealing, don't improve the comfort of the saddle for horse or rider.

# New or Used

When purchasing a new saddle, you can order or buy specifically what you want. Many brand-name saddles "off the rack" offer several design options, while a custom saddlemaker can build almost anything. However, there are many good used saddles on the market, and one may be right for you.

If you are considering a used saddle, here's what to check for.

1/ *Overall quality.* If it looks worn out and used up, it probably isn't worth buying and trying to fix up.

2/ *Broken tree.* Set the saddle upright, with the horn and gullet toward the floor. Push down on the cantle several times. If you feel a lot of give, or if the saddle seems to pop, the tree is probably broken. Look underneath the saddle; you may be able to see a break in the tree. Or lay the saddle on its side and push down, against the bars, to see if there's lots of give.

3/ *Rigging.* Be sure it hangs evenly from either side of the saddle. Look at the saddle, with the stirrups tied up, from both the front and the rear to see if the rigging drops evenly on both sides. Look from above, down toward the saddle seat, to see if the rings are evenly positioned from front to rear on the saddle. If the rigging doesn't seem balanced, the saddle will be hard to position correctly on a horse's back.

4/ *Condition of the leather.* Is it dry and cracked, or supple and flexible? Worn latigos and off-billets aren't that difficult or expensive to replace, but worn and dried-out rigging leather means a major repair job.

5/ *Stitching.* Is the saddle well-stitched throughout? Poor stitching with poor quality material quickly unravels the construction of any saddle. If staples have been used in place of stitching, do not buy the saddle.

6/ *Stirrup leathers.* Do they show wear, or are they relatively sound? Replacing worn stirrup leathers is not as easy or inexpensive as replacing a broken latigo, but not as difficult or expensive as repairing faulty rigging.

## Pads and Blankets

Materials for saddle pads and blankets include everything from natural fibers, such as cotton and wool, to synthetic fleeces and foams—all in a variety of colors and patterns. However fashionable the top layer of a pad or blanket, what is next to a horse's back is what counts.

1/ *Wool.* For years, a 100-percent wool, woven Navajo-type blanket has been favored by many horsemen, who like the natural fiber next to their horses' backs. The tighter the weave, the more durable and heavier the blanket, and as a wool blanket absorbs sweat, it becomes even heavier. Too, care must be taken in washing wool blankets, which might fade or shrink.

2/ *Cotton.* Although lighter in weight than wool, cotton blankets are not as sturdy and lasting as wool ones, especially for everyday use.

3/ *Horsehair.* Another natural fiber, horsehair has long been used in making saddle pads. What could be more natural and less irritating to a horse than hair on hair? Horsehair pads are quite durable, although somewhat heavy, and offer less choice in style and color.

4/ *Fleece and fleece-lined.* These pads, often topped with brightly colored fabrics, provide ample cushioning for a horse's back. However, caution must be used to ensure that no twigs or burrs become stuck in the fleece and later sore a horse's back. Fleece pads, available in 100-percent wool or synthetic fibers, tend to slip more on a horse's back, for example, than would a felt pad.

5/ *Felt.* Wool is also the top choice for making felt pads, although synthetic felts are on the market. A thin felt pad of $\frac{3}{8}$-inch thickness, for example, can be used under an expensive Navajo show blanket, to protect it from dirt and sweat. Such a thin pad washes easily in the machine. Much thicker felt pads, available for everyday use, are also available.

6/ *Foam.* Dense, closed-cell foam pads provide a lot of cushion with little bulk, and foam absorbs shock well, too. It does not, however, absorb sweat well. Many horsemen prefer a combination pad of dense foam sandwiched between layers of felt. The foam cushions the shock, and the natural wool felt absorbs a horse's sweat.

Blankets and pads last longer when cleaned periodically. Woven Navajo blankets are best taken to the dry cleaner. Other blankets and pads benefit from regular washing, even if only with cold water from the hose, to remove caked-in dirt and salt from sweat. A high-pressure hose at a carwash works well, too.

If you use soap on a blanket or pad, be sure to rinse thoroughly, so the soap does not irritate a horse's back. Fleece pads can be difficult to clean. Before hosing the fleece, use a currycomb or dog grooming brush to pick the fleece clean.

## Halters and Leads

Halters are made from rope, flat nylon webbing, or leather, with sizing descriptions such as large horse, regular or average horse, small horse, yearling, pony, or weanling. Most halters offer limited adjustment.

Rope halters, often made of a synthetic material, such as rot-resistant round nylon, are durable and inexpensive.

Halters made from flat nylon webbing are stout and usually have brass-plated hardware. The weight and width of the nylon webbing varies and may be single- or double-ply. Such halters may even have a felt lining.

Leather halters are designed much the same and range from the serviceably plain stable halter to the silver-trimmed show halter.

Leads range in length from 6½ feet to 10 feet or more, usually with a bolt snap or bull snap at one end. Cotton rope leads, either braided or twisted, are available in varying diameters, as are leads of round nylon. Flat nylon webbing and leather are also used for leads.

Should a horse set back and pull against you, nylon webbing, rope, and leather can burn your hand far worse than can cotton rope.

Some leads have a stud chain on one end. The chain, from 18-36 inches in length, can be run through the noseband rings on the halter and over the horse's nose to give the handler added control. The use of a stud chain is not restricted to stallions.

When selecting a halter and lead, feel the different weights of rope, webbing, or leather used. Check the snaps and buckles. Remember that a halter and lead are only as stout as their hardware. A halter made of the stoutest nylon webbing is no good if it has cheap, "pot-metal" hardware. The same holds true for a lead rope. A rope stout enough to tie up a battleship is worthless if it has a 10-cent snap. Heavy-duty brass hardware is best.

Your halter and lead will see much use, and you are relying on their strength and durability to ensure that your horse stays where you tie him. If a horse succeeds in breaking loose, he can often be injured if he flips over when the halter or lead breaks. And, breaking loose once can result in him trying to break loose again, a very bad habit.

# Bridles and Reins

Bridles, or headstalls, come in two styles: a browband, or a one-ear, which is formed by a slot in the crown piece or by a sliding earpiece attached to the crown. Browband bridles have a throatlatch that buckles or snaps, as do some one-ear bridles. A throatlatch can help prevent a horse from rubbing off his bridle. Which style headstall to use is primarily a matter of personal preference.

Bridles made of leather can be decorated with silver trim or rawhide braid to match any saddle. Flat-braided nylon is popular for headgear as well since it is more sweat-resistant than leather. Curb straps are made of leather, nylon, or chain. Often a chain curb is used in combination with nylon or leather straps.

Split reins are two separate reins. A roping rein is one continuous rein attached to the bit rings, often with a snap for convenience. Reins with a romal are usually made of braided leather; where the two reins join together, the romal is attached.

Reins can be made of flat leather, braided leather, webbed nylon, and such, and vary in width from less than ½ inch to more than 1 inch. Length in split reins ranges from about 6 feet to 8 feet or more. Reins can be attached to the bit with a snap, a Conway buckle, Chicago screws, a twist-loop, a quick-change loop, or leather ties.

A word of caution: If your bridle has Chicago screws, be aware that some screws are simply too short to adequately bind together several layers of leather. The solution: Purchase longer screws at a hardware store or saddle shop to ensure that your bridle and bit, or bit and reins, stay attached. Also applying a dab of clear nail polish or glue to the screws will help keep them tight. Because Chicago screws tend to work loose, some horsemen prefer leather ties instead.

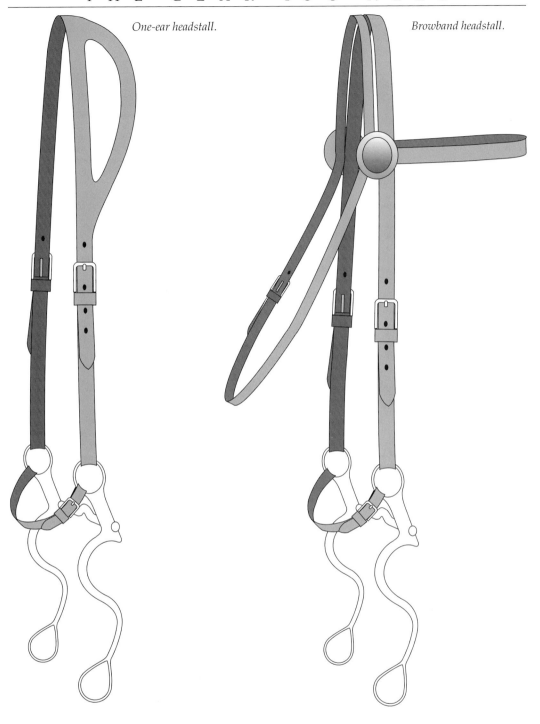

*One-ear headstall.*

*Browband headstall.*

Whatever you use, check the screws, leather ties, or other fastenings on your bridle, to be sure they are sound and snug, for safety's sake. Remember, too, that a horse often sweats along his neck, which makes the reins, particularly those of leather, a prime target for deterioration. You rely on headgear to control your horse, so make sure your bridle is sturdy and safe.

## Bits and Hackamores

Don't feel badly if the array of bits on the tack shop wall overwhelms you; even

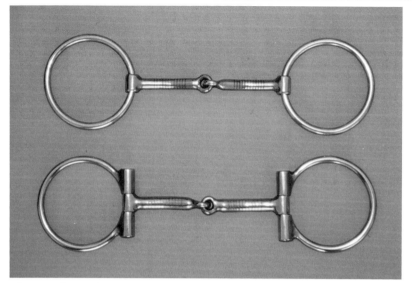

*The upper bit is a loose-or O-ring snaffle, and the ring rotates freely at the butt of the mouthpiece. The lower bit is a fixed-ring snaffle and has no rotation. The stripes on the mouthpieces are inlaid copper, which helps salivation. When a horse salivates, his jaws are more relaxed and less resistant.*

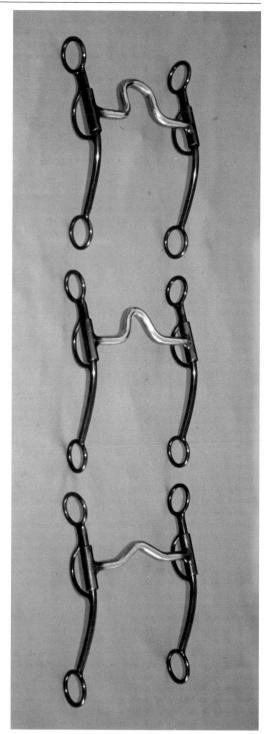

*These three are curb bits with loose, rather than fixed, shanks. There are differences, however, in the mouthpiece designs. The middle rings on each shank are for attaching another pair of reins, not the curb chain.*

experienced horsemen are often bamboozled by bits.

Generally, bits are described as either snaffle bits or shanked bits, called curb bits. Snaffle bits usually have a jointed mouthpiece, attached to an O-ring or a D-ring, and do not have leverage action. Most young horses are bitted for the first time with a snaffle. Curb bits, with curb straps attached, use leverage to control a horse.

Bits are made from any number of metals and alloys—sweet iron, stainless steel, aluminum, and such. The bit may or may not have copper or sweet iron in the mouthpiece, both of which encourage salivation to ensure more comfort as the horse carries the bit. The bit shanks may be plain or engraved, or even overlaid with silver.

There are two kinds of hackamores—bosal hackamores and mechanical hackamores. The term hackamore describes the headstall, with bosal and mechanical referring to the type of control device

THE GEAR YOU NEED

*This is a hackamore with a rawhide bosal, often used for training young horses. A horsehair mecate is attached.*

attached to the headstall. A bosal, or noseband, is usually made of braided rawhide, leather, or plain rope. It's often used in working young horses. Hackamore reins used with a bosal are usually mecate-style and made of horsehair or cotton rope. A mecate is a continuous length of horsehair or rope attached to form a single rein that loops around the horse's neck. The additional length can be tied to the saddle horn or tucked under the rider's belt; if he falls off, he can grab it to hold onto the horse, preventing a long walk home.

A mechanical hackamore has a nosepiece, two metal shanks, and a curb strap or chain. It operates on leverage. The nose piece can be leather or covered chain, for example, and the metal parts may be aluminum, stainless steel, or chrome-plated. Mechanical hackamores are not designed for training colts. They are best suited for broke horses. Mechanical hackamores are often used in timed events or by heavy-handed riders who continually bump a horse's sensitive mouth when using a bit.

## Miscellaneous Gear

Tie-downs, cavessons, martingales, breast collars, and protective leg gear are most commonly used.

A tie-down strap attaches to the D-ring on the front cinch and to a noseband, separate from the bridle. Tie-downs are often used to minimize the effects of head-slinging, or to aid a competition horse in balancing during fast, tight maneuvers.

A cavesson is simply a noseband, often put on a young horse during the bitting process to discourage him from opening his mouth as he becomes accustomed to carrying a bit.

The running martingale is a training device that attaches to the cinch, between the horse's legs, and has two forks, each with a ring at the end, through which the reins are placed. This martingale, when

*A running martingale should only be used with a snaffle bit. This horse is also equipped with splint and bell boots.*

adjusted correctly, goes into effect to correct a horse's headset only when the horse moves his head up to an unacceptable position. Western riders sometimes call running martingales cowboy training forks.

Breast collars often are a necessity to ensure that a saddle doesn't slide on a horse's back during strenuous work. A trail rider, traveling up and down hills all day, often uses a breast collar for this reason, just as a cowboy working cattle does. Also, a breast collar can help stabilize the saddle on a mutton-withered horse. In the show ring, although not mandatory, breast collars are often coordinated with the bridle and saddle to give an exhibitor a polished appearance.

Splint boots wrap around a horse's front cannon bones and help protect his legs from a sharp blow during fast maneuvers, such as spins.

Skid boots are placed over the back fetlocks to prevent them from becoming burned or skinned during a sliding stop or rollback.

Bell boots protect the coronet band during events such as barrel racing, roping, or reining when one front foot might strike the opposite one, or a hind foot might hit a front foot. Combination boots include the protection offered by both splint and bell boot.

Protective leg gear materials include leather, lined leather, synthetic foams, felts, rubber, and plastics; these are now available in many colors. The fastenings on splint, skid, or bell boots can be

anything from buckles to VELCRO®.

Leg gear, breast collars, and martingales all are no different from any other piece of equipment in that regular cleaning and conditioning affect how long the gear will last. Dirt and sweat not only contribute to deterioration, but also affect how comfortable the equipment is to use.

In addition to cleaning gear, it's also a good idea to use a conditioner on leather equipment. Many conditioning products are on the market, such as pure neatsfoot oil, which is beneficial to use, but will darken the leather. So, before you condition your new saddle, ask your tack dealer or shoe repairman about the product you plan to use.

You have your first horse now and the gear to ride him. The next step is developing the good horsemanship to safely enjoy the experience.

# PARTNERING UP

**9**

AT LAST, your new horse is home; you're ready to enjoy your new sport and your new companion. And you do . . . for a few days or a week or two. Then you realize that your first horse has become a dictator, insisting that you do things his way or not at all.

What's the problem? Why haven't you been able to partner up with your new buddy, who was a well-behaved horse when you test-rode him? You envisioned a wonderful experience each day at the barn, and it hasn't materialized.

Perhaps the horse turns his rear toward you when you catch him, even though that wasn't the case during your pre-purchase ride. When you're afoot, he may be leading you, rather than you leading him. Perhaps you're having trouble riding your new horse away from the barn. These are not uncommon problems for a novice horseman.

Granted, there are a few outlaw horses and many young unbroke or unschooled horses with whom it is difficult to establish discipline and order, but they don't fit the profile of the mature, broke, first horse

*For better interaction between horse and rider, the person needs to have some understanding of the horse's point of view.*

under discussion here. However, even a well-trained, grown, broke horse will get sluggish and lazy if he can get away with it.

Think about your initial test-ride on this horse. He was well-behaved and responsive, which was why you wanted him in the first place. He responded well to you and the handler, who communicated his expectations to the horse in a way the horse could understand. The handler's consistency in communication contributed much toward the horse's responsiveness.

It's probable that the seller had more experience with horses than you. The seller felt more sure of himself and confident of his actions than you probably feel when you handle your first horse. Accept it, if that's the case, but recognize that your situation need not stay that way.

As a matter of fact, it won't. Your ability to work with your horse will get better or worse, but it won't stay the same. Whether things get better or get worse is up to you. But you can meet the challenge and improve the relationship with your horse; after all, you're the human with the greater understanding and reasoning ability.

Horses have been described as sociable herd animals, and with good reason. An individual horse found protection within the herd as his species evolved; those horses who could live within the social order of the herd survived.

Even though mankind has taken the horse from his herd environment in the wild, a blueprint for operating within such a social order remains part of a horse's makeup. He finds his place within his herd's social order to this day. He may move up in the herd's standings by challenging and dominating a less assertive, more submissive horse. Or he may be put in his place by a more dominant, assertive animal. This holds true even for the lone horse whose herd consists of two—the horse and the human who handles him.

Whether it's a real horse herd of 25 or a mixed-species herd of 2, as the horse sees it, each herd has its leader. The leader claims his position through dominance, not necessarily abuse, of the other herd members. When his position is challenged, the leader quickly reestablishes order within the herd or loses his position.

*Pinned ears and bared teeth are commonplace among pastured horses as they determine pecking order in the herd. The same behavior, however, is unacceptable when a horse learns to relate to a human as herd boss.*

A herd boss makes decisions, for example, about where the herd takes its rest or when the herd goes on the move, and herd members follow his lead.

Even in the herd of two, a horse looks to the established herd boss for guidance. If you don't establish your position as herd boss, your horse will assume the leadership role. This holds true until his position in the social order is changed by a more dominant, assertive herd member—you. Now you're beginning to grasp how your first horse relates to you.

The change in your horse's responsiveness, when you got him home, was probably a gradual one. Think about what happened when he failed to respond as you expected. Maybe he appeared a little bit mad and ready to fight you, or a little bit scared and ready to run from you.

That's known as fight or flight in the horse world, and such behavior also ties to the evolution of the horse. He is a grazing animal, rather than a carnivore; the horse is a prey animal. This meant he was victim to such predators as lions and tigers. When attacked, often by the predator jumping onto his back, the horse had two choices. He could choose flight and, perhaps, avoid the predator. Or a horse could fight, using his teeth to bite his attacker and his feet to paw and kick him.

Fight or flight is still a part of the modern-day horse. Many horses, when challenged, are apt to practice flight and avoid a fight. Even though some are more dominant within the herd than others, horses are generally soft-natured animals, rather than aggressive, warlike ones. Their faith in the herd boss is such that, with the appropriate domination, most horses will accept a potentially frightening situation. And they do so, even though such acceptance may run counter to their natural instincts.

Consider that, through centuries of

74

evolution, the horse most feared a predator such as a lion landing on his back. Yet, for years the horse has allowed man to sit there, even swinging a rope or firing a gun, without responding to an innate need to flee.

Remember the horse's accepting nature as you assert yourself as boss of the herd. Understand that assertiveness is not the same as abuse, yet both can be used to dominate. By asserting control, even if occasionally in a more aggressive manner, you dominate the horse. But you also have a herd-mate who believes in your leadership and one who will serve you. When you dominate through abuse, the moment the horse has the opportunity to flee, he will.

Unless you assert control of your first horse, your riding and horse-handling experiences are not likely to be safe ones. A large dog can run over you, so to speak, and possibly knock you down, but it's unlikely you will be significantly hurt by the experience. A 1,000-pound horse who runs over you, or away with you, can hurt you.

For safety's sake, establish yourself as the herd boss, the one to whom the horse gives ground, rather than vice versa. The horse must watch you and respect your space, rather than demanding that you get out of his territory. Asserting control is sometimes difficult, especially when you are a novice horseman, who often feels uncertain about how to go about things.

In recent years, the word dominance has become associated with abuse of one sort or another, but it originally meant to command or control, with no mention of abuse.

Command can be established by a person with a dominant character or personality. It is also established by a person with a dominant mind-set. Your first horse can sense your uncertainty, just as he can sense weakness in any herd boss. On the other hand, your horse cannot tell if you are innately dominant in your character or if you have consciously chosen to act dominant.

You may have simply decided, "Today, I take control; nothing less is acceptable." Even though you consider yours a less-than-dominant nature, you realize that you must be herd boss. Good horsemanship is something of a head game. You must act as a leader before you can sell your horse on the idea that you are the boss.

Remember: A horse can accept being dominated; it's a part of his makeup. Even better, he is a forgiving animal. You can dominate him and still put him to good use, once he has accepted his position. In addition, you can establish a rapport with him, just as you do a longtime friend. But you cannot accomplish any of this without first having his respect.

Although this is not a horse training book, there are concepts that can help you feel more confident and in control of your first horse. Once you understand a few basic ideas, you'll be better prepared to enjoy a trip to the barn. Here are some tools you can use.

Asserting control over your first horse is not as difficult if you approach each challenge with one thing in mind. Make the right response easier for your horse to deliver, and the wrong response harder to accomplish.

Whatever the problem, stop and think how to make the right thing easy, and the wrong thing hard. Hard does not mean abusive in this context; it means difficult, and it means tougher on the horse than it is on you.

In years past, horses were bucked out to accustom them to riders on their backs and were forced to submit to human handlers. In recent years, however, horsemen have approached handling their mounts with more finesse, teaching a horse to accept domination, rather than forcing him to do so.

**Make the right response easier for your horse to deliver, and the wrong response harder to accomplish.**

Take, for example, the young horse in the round pen who doesn't want to be caught. Nowadays, rather than rope and snub him to a post so a person can handle him, a horseman might keep the young horse moving around the pen, physically exerting himself. Periodically, the man stops and approaches the horse, or even waits a moment, to let a horse approach him. If that doesn't happen, the horse is put back on the move, but not to the point of exhaustion. He simply receives no rest from steady work until he accepts a human's approach.

This way of establishing leadership as herd boss is more time-consuming—at first. But after a few days, the horse learns he has nothing to fear. It's easier to let you handle him than it is to stay on the move. So he becomes easier to catch, rather than fleeing human control. More examples of making the right thing easy and the wrong thing hard are in the chapter about problems with horses.

Another tool often used by horsemen nowadays is desensitization. This term describes a method of accustoming a horse to something that may frighten him. You discover, for example, that the broke horse you test-rode is scared of your rain gear. The vinyl poncho or slicker flaps noisily in the wind.

Rather than forcing a horse to accept the slicker, a horseman teaches him that it's harmless by gradually approaching the horse. A horse indicates uneasiness or stress by flaring his nostrils, for example, or gathering himself to bolt. Recognizing those clues, the horseman pauses a moment, reassuring the horse. The horse learns that a slicker 5 feet away is harm-less, and he no longer fears it. Again, by reading the horse's reactions, a horseman recognizes acceptance. So, the man brings the slicker closer, again pausing when he recognizes signs of uneasiness.

Desensitization is a give-and-take process. The horse slowly becomes accustomed to the noisy slicker and accepts it as harmless. This process, too, seems time-consuming at first, but pays big dividends in the long run.

Another concept has been utilized in the two previous cases—repetition and reward. In both instances, the horse was presented with the same situation—repeatedly. At any indication of acceptance, he was rewarded, either by relief from work or by reassurance from his herd boss, the horseman.

Here's a basic example of repetition and reward. A rider says whoa, pulls on, then releases the reins when a horse stops. The horse has learned through repetition that, if he gives the right or easy response, he gets a reward and receives slack in the reins.

As you handle your first horse more, there will be times when he is not as responsive as you would like. When that happens, think your way through the situation, before you ride him through it. You'll be more successful and add to your stature as herd boss in the process. In addition, you'll find a more willing companion in your horse, one who feels safe and secure. He understands his position within the herd because you have taught him what it is.

Remember, too, that any novice can benefit from riding instruction. The better he can control his horse, the less likely the horse is to take advantage of his rider. For more information, see the chapter on lessons and trainers.

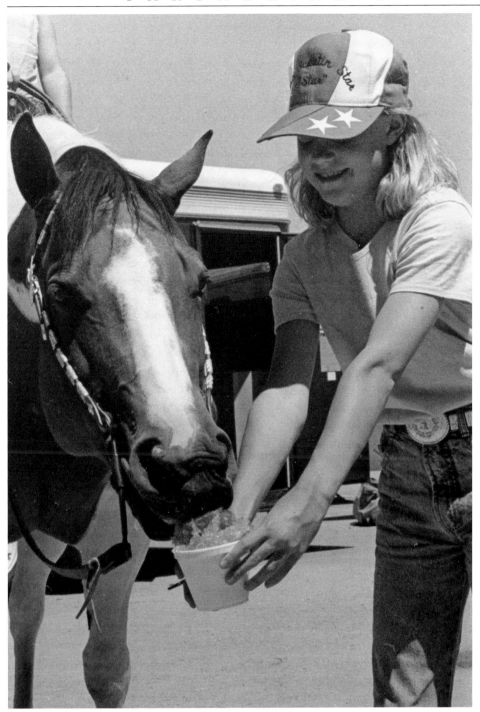

Here's a pair who have partnered up. Jenna Peterson of Kent, Wash., and her mount, Ima Scootin Star, have the kind of relationship most first-time horse owners would envy. The pair were competing in the American Junior Paint Horse Association World Championship Show in Reno, Nev., when this photo was taken. At this level of competition, a horse must respect his handler as the boss—even if she is "just a girl." But, it's just the girl who enjoys sharing a snow cone in a cup with her horse.

# HANDLING YOUR HORSE WHEN YOU'RE AFOOT

## 10

MAINTAINING control of your horse when you're afoot is one of the most effective aids to help you become a successful horseman. Remember, when you and the horse are a herd of two, you're the boss. It should make no difference to the horse if you're on his back or at the end of his lead.

So use the time when you're working afoot as an opportunity to reinforce your position of leadership. Establish your presence in his world, and in a way he can relate to, from the ground. You'll become more confident before you ever mount up, and your horse will become more secure, recognizing you as a strong herd boss, and being less apt to challenge your authority.

You wouldn't let a large dog shove you around or knock you down, but if you did, you probably wouldn't be hurt badly. However, a 1,000-pound horse who shoves you around can hurt you. Maintaining his respect is your number-one priority, for safety's sake.

## Making the Approach

When you're afoot, always speak to your horse so that he is aware of your presence. He will come to recognize your voice as time goes by, and become more secure and relaxed in your presence.

Approach a horse by moving toward his shoulder, rather than approaching directly from the rear. A horse can see you better when you approach from the front or the side. His vision to the rear is nearly nonexistent unless he turns his head.

Therefore, never approach a horse in the blind spot directly behind him. Should

*Maintaining control over a horse is as important when you're afoot as it is when you're in the saddle.*

it be necessary, for whatever reason, to move around behind a horse, speak and make your presence known. If you don't speak, and startle him, a horse may revert to flight or fight, which in this case may include a kick aimed at you.

Also realize that a horse cannot see directly below his head. It's particularly hard for a horse to be aware of a small child's presence. The child should speak to signify his presence or, better yet, alter his angle of approach, toward the horse's better field of vision.

Too, a horse sometimes senses motion faster than he can identify what caused the motion. A sudden movement may startle him, before he determines what or who caused the motion. In this case, one soothing word from a familiar voice often reassures a horse that an unexpected movement is not a threatening one.

Deliberate actions on your part are also reassuring to a horse. Try not to act timid or hesitant around your new horse. He will sense your uncertainty and grow uneasy himself, which will make you, in turn, even more uncomfortable. The cycle can repeat itself and escalate if unchecked. So be straightforward in your approach. Act as if you are sure of what your doing. Assurance, even when it's assumed, better enables you to build a rapport with your new companion, than will timidity.

# Catching Your Horse

Many people use repetition and reward to facilitate catching a horse, particularly one in pasture. They use a catch pen or loafing shed in the pasture for routine feeding, and the horse is easier to catch in the more confined area. The grain reinforces the idea that entering the pen can be a pleasant experience.

Use a handful or two of grain if it isn't a regular feeding time. If it is, let the horse have a small portion of his daily ration before catching and riding him. Many people also use a distinct whistle daily at feeding time, and the horse learns to associate the whistle with his grain and is more apt to come.

If yours is a stabled horse, catching him shouldn't be a problem—unless he repeatedly turns his hind end to you. A horse should face up, as it's called; this means he should turn and face you, giving you the attention and respect you deserve. Stalled

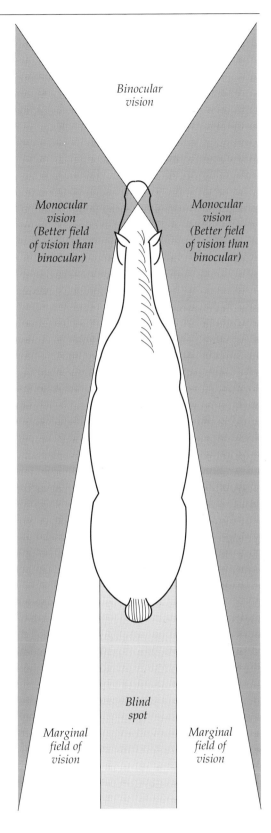

Binocular vision

Monocular vision (Better field of vision than binocular)

Monocular vision (Better field of vision than binocular)

Blind spot

Marginal field of vision

Marginal field of vision

*The safest place to approach a horse is from the side, where his vision is better, not from behind where his vision is limited or nonexistent.*

horses often are easily caught since that means they get a break from the monotony and a change of scenery.

Whether catching a horse in a catch pen or stall, always try to maintain your position at his shoulder. You can take a step forward or back, as necessary, to either block

*1/ This series of five photographs shows a handler approaching and haltering a horse in the pasture. In this case, a little grain in the bucket ensures that the horse finds the experience a pleasant one, and therefore he is easy to catch.*

his forward motion or to make him face you, where his head is more accessible.

## Learning His Language

Learn to read a horse's body language when you approach. His response generally indicates acceptance, fear, or aggression.

A relaxed, calm demeanor means his world is in order. The boss is coming, and the horse is comfortable in that knowledge and accepting of it.

Fear can result in acceptance, flight, or fight. A horse can be fearful of his handler, yet submissive to his leadership. In this case, a horse faces up, but his body language indicates fear, uneasiness, or timidity. It's up to the handler to reward a horse for facing up and to alleviate his fear. Fear can lead to flight when a horse is in a pasture or catch pen with room enough to run. In a stall, there's little room for flight, so a horse who is afraid might take a defensive position, ready to kick. Aggressive behavior, such as turning his hind end to you, can mean a horse is preparing to kick . . . to challenge your authority, which is unacceptable. Should you be challenged in such a manner, move immediately to reestablish your leadership. If

you're uncertain of how to go about it, get an experienced horseman to help you safely approach the problem.

Sometimes a mildly aggressive move on your part, such as deliberately flipping the end of your lead rope (from a distance) toward a horse's hind end, is enough to convince a horse that facing you is the better alternative. This method sometimes can work with a fearful horse as well as an aggressive one.

Too, the method for catching a horse described in the previous chapter, where a horse is kept busy unless or until he faces up, can help you establish control. Unless you have had a lot of experience with horses, it's best to work under the guidance of an experienced horseman at first. You'll probably get more immediate results, and he can show you how to master the more effective techniques safely.

## Haltering Your Horse

Once you have entered a stall or pen, move deliberately toward your horse's near shoulder, speaking as you approach. As you draw closer, rub him on the neck or shoulder. Then use whatever method works best for you to halter him.

Some people wrap their right arm over a horse's neck, reaching under the throatlatch to grasp the halter and put it on.

2/ The handler, Sarah Pulliam, let the horse have a few oats, then slipped the lead rope around his neck.

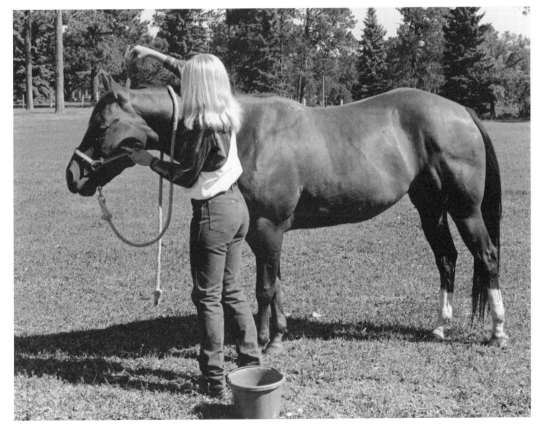

3/ While haltering him, Sarah puts the bucket down.

4/ *The horse stands quietly.*

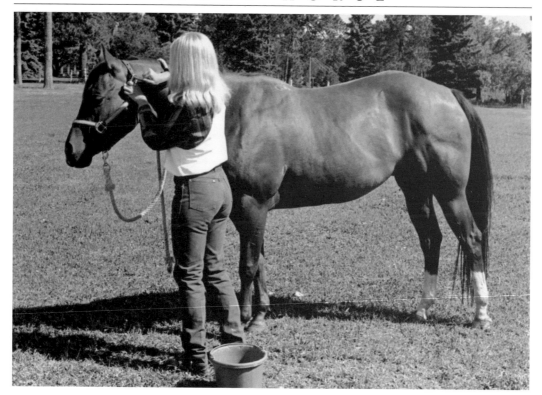

5/ *After buckling the halter, Sarah lets the horse have more oats. Being this easy to catch is an invaluable trait.*

Others approach from underneath, with both hands on the halter, and slip it onto a horse's head. Some people carry a halter in the left hand, with the tail of the lead rope in their right. As they rub a horse's neck, they drop the lead over the neck and grasp it underneath, maintaining a hold until the halter is in place. Do whatever you are most comfortable with.

Never, in any case, wrap a lead rope or halter around your arm, or tie or buckle such gear around your waist. That's asking for trouble should something startle the horse.

Sooner or later, everyone experiences a little difficulty in haltering a horse. Something unexpected may surprise him, just as you're about to fasten the halter, and before you can reassure him, a horse resorts to flight. And some horses do learn to be wily and evasive when it comes to being haltered. Don't worry about the occasional difficulty in catching or haltering your horse. But watch for a pattern developing if you repeatedly have trouble. Study what happens and work to change the pattern. Determine a way to make the right response easy for the horse, and the wrong response more difficult.

Take care when turning your horse loose, too. Lead him into a stall or pasture, turning him around so you have access to the gate or stall door, before you take off the halter. Do remove the halter. No matter how convenient it seems to leave a halter on a loose horse, a horse wearing a halter, sooner or later, will catch it on a fence post, tree limb, hydrant, or such. Horses have been seriously injured or killed as a result.

# Leading Your Horse

Position yourself to lead your horse by standing a little ahead of his left shoulder. Although a horse should lead from either side, most horses are more accustomed to being led from the left. When handling a strange horse, it's best to start from that side. After you become more familiar with your horse, you can check his response when leading him from the right side.

Standing at his left, grasp the lead in your right hand, about 12 inches from the halter, holding the excess length in your left hand. Some people coil the lead rope in the left hand, but this is dangerous. Should a horse set back and pull against you, the coils can tighten, and the lead then burns your hand. In a worst-case scenario, you may be dragged if the horse runs off.

A better way to carry excess lead is to open your left hand, palm up, and double the extra length across it. Should anything unexpected occur, you can open your hand and drop the excess length entirely.

Should a horse pull away from you unexpectedly, drop your right hand from the lead to avoid being jerked off your feet. Try to hold the lead with your left hand. The lead should feed smoothly between your left thumb and index finger because it was doubled in your palm, not coiled around your hand. You can sometimes take a firm grip on the lead, bringing your left hand around behind you, below your left hip, to brace against the pull, and prevent the horse from getting loose.

Once you're in position to lead your horse, use a cue to indicate that forward motion is desired. Many people cluck; others say "walk." Whatever your cue, the more consistently you use it, the more consistently your horse will learn to respond.

Remember that a horse reads your body language, too. If you amble in no particular direction, he will also. Step out purposefully when you lead your horse, briskly and attentively. You're the boss; your horse will probably follow your lead. Keep your eyes forward, looking ahead to your destination. Later, when you're riding, you will need to develop the habit of looking ahead of your horse, not down, at the ground. So use the opportunity, when you lead him, to practice. Do glance underfoot periodically, but don't habitually look down.

# Rushing Ahead and Lagging Back

Your horse's body should travel a path parallel to yours. He should not stray onto your path of travel, but maintain a respectful distance from you. He should not charge ahead of you, nor should he lag behind. His attention should be on you, not a

*Both the horse and han-
dler shown here are alert
and attentive. The handler
is correctly positioned,
and the horse appears to be
alert and responsive.*

*Because the handler is
somewhat relaxed and in-
attentive as she leads this
horse, the horse's response
seems to be equally relaxed,
with a lack of focus on the
handler.*

clump of fresh green grass off to the right.

When a horse forges ahead of you, get his attention by using a short, quick snatch on the lead. Don't pull on the lead; a horse usually pulls back harder, and you can't out-pull a horse. But he often will respond to a quick snap of the wrist, followed by a release of the pressure. If he doesn't, give the lead a harder, quicker snap with your wrist.

The same technique usually works when a horse's attention drifts from you to grass, or any distraction. A few quick snaps of the wrist, and he should focus again on you.

A horse who lags at the end of a lead is no fun either. One horse may lag behind his handler at a walk. Another may well walk alongside his handler, but drag on the lead at the trot. Whatever the problem, first be sure that you are cueing the horse properly and not restricting his movement with your right hand. Remember to step forward briskly as you cue for forward motion.

It may be necessary to use a long whip to reinforce the cue for forward motion. Grasp the whip in your left hand, with the handle pointing forward, and hold the whip parallel with the horse's body. Cue the horse as you step forward. If he lags behind, snap your left wrist to bring the end of the whip toward his rump, to encourage forward motion.

Be cautious when you do this and businesslike in your approach. If you are too timid with your action, a horse may think the end of the whip is a pesky fly and try to kick it away. If you are too aggressive in your reinforcement of the cue, a horse may react defensively, again, by kicking. This technique, at first, is best practiced under the supervision of an experienced horseman.

Traveling with you, at whatever speed you're going, means a horse has rate, as it's called. He rates his speed according to yours. Later, when you're mounted, you also will expect your horse to rate his speed. The vocal commands will probably be much the same. However, the pressure on the lead will translate into pressure on the reins.

# Establish Your Territory

Your best safeguard, when handling a horse afoot, is teaching him to maintain a respectful distance from your body. A critical point: He must understand that he cannot enter your territory without your permission. For him to do otherwise puts him in the position of leadership. You, however, as the boss, can enter his territory, and he must give ground and be submissive when you do.

One way to help establish that understanding takes only a few minutes but, done regularly, yields results. Stand near your horse's left shoulder, facing his side. Use your right thumb, or the handle of a grooming tool, for example, and push against the horse's lower side, about where your foot would hang in the stirrup. A horse's instinctive reaction is to push back, into your hand. This is somewhat a challenge to your authority because he has failed to submit and yield ground to his herd boss.

Don't lose patience; try again, and again, and again. Remember, he instinctively wants to push back, rather than yield to the pressure. All you want, at this point, is for the horse to take one step away from you, even if he only untracks his hind legs. If pushing on his side does not seem to have any effect, try bumping his side repeatedly.

Once he has taken a step, rub him or do something to indicate that he has pleased you. Move around to his right-hand side and do the same thing. Don't quit until he has taken that first step, and reward him when he does. Do this several times from both sides.

The next day, repeat the procedure, asking him to take a step or two on each side. Don't quit until you have received an appropriate response. The third day, push on his sides some more, asking him to give more ground to you. Over a short period of time, your horse will learn that, when you step toward him, he steps away from you, yielding ground to you.

**Longeing a horse involves doing one of two things: You are either herding the horse or heading him off.**

This becomes a method of correction when your horse steps into your territory. When leading him, for example, if he tries to make you get out of his way, use the same push on his side to remind him that he respects your territory and steps away from you.

Learning to yield to the pressure of your thumb is ground work that also translates effectively when you make the transition to riding. You will use your feet in much the same way as your thumb, to cue your horse for different maneuvers when you're mounted. So you reap a double benefit.

## Say Whoa and Mean It

Whoa is the command to stop. It means the same from the ground as it does from the saddle. Once stopped, your horse should stand quietly until you indicate otherwise. Don't accept anything less than a complete halt and a quiet stance. You're building in a safeguard for future use. A correct response to whoa may save you from serious difficulty later, for example, should a curb strap break when you're riding.

Every time you lead your horse and stop him, use the command whoa; reinforce it with a quick snap of the lead if necessary. Once your horse stops, relax yourself, to encourage quietness in the horse. Make whoa a pleasant experience to him; he gets to rest then.

If your horse doesn't stand quietly, firmly tell him whoa again, giving an another snap of the lead. Yelling whoa more loudly won't help, and generally adds to a horse's uneasiness. Don't stand tensely either, anticipating that your horse won't remain quiet. He will feed off your tension and be even less likely to stay put.

Patiently reinforcing the cue to stand still does eventually bring results, especially when you take a matter-of-fact approach toward schooling your horse. After all, he didn't fail to stand quietly to spite you. More likely he was responding instinctively, for example, to the approach of another horse, or the urge to snatch some green grass. Whatever the situation, don't quit working with your horse until he stands. When you quit in frustration, you allow him to control you, and he becomes the boss.

## Reading Your Horse

One of the best ways to learn about your horse and how he responds to certain actions is to turn him into a fairly small area, such as a catch pen or round pen. After he becomes comfortable in his new location, step into the pen. Approach him, move around him, retreat from him, and study his response. This time together, especially at first, better enables you to read his body language. You'll begin to learn the signs that indicate when he is uneasy or accepting of a situation, or if he's issuing a challenge. Again, ask an experienced horseman for assistance. He can show you how to avoid taking unnecessary risks.

## Longeing Your Horse

Another effective method of working your horse from the ground is to longe him. A handler attaches a long lead, or longe line, to the halter, and the horse moves on a circle around the handler.

Many horses are familiar with the longeing routine since it is often part of a young horse's training. Longeing is an excellent way to settle down a stall-fresh horse before riding him or to exercise a horse who can't be ridden; perhaps, he has a sore back or a gall from the cinch. A horse can be longed with or without being saddled.

The longe line is usually about 25 to 30 feet long, which means the circle has a diameter about double the line's length.

Many people also use a long whip, which is no more severe than the hand using it. In this case, the whip becomes an extension of the handler's arm, safely enabling him to reinforce a cue without placing himself in a precarious position.

It's also a good idea to wear gloves to prevent a rope burn, should a horse unexpectedly pull back or whirl and go the other way. As with a lead, never tie or wrap a longe line around your body, hand, or arm in such a way that you can be fouled in the line.

Longeing is best mastered when working in a round pen or smaller catch pen. Use the same cues as for leading a horse— a cluck to move forward, and the vocal command whoa to stop. This time, however, you are establishing your leadership by working at some distance from your horse. When starting to longe, it's sometimes easier to work a horse without using the full length of the line, until control has been established.

Longeing a horse involves doing one of two things: You are either herding the horse or heading him off. After all, such is the herd boss's job. Whenever you step ahead of a horse's shoulder, when he's on the line, you are cutting him off or blocking his forward motion. By positioning yourself behind his shoulder, you are driving him forward. The farther you, at the end of a longe line, drop back alongside a horse, the harder you are driving him, so to speak.

To longe a horse in a left-hand circle, hold the line in your left hand, gathering the excess safely, just as you would excess lead rope. Carry the longe whip in your right hand. Many people carry the excess line in their right hand, along with the longe whip. To work a horse to the right, reverse hands, holding the line in your right and the whip in your left.

Cue the horse for forward motion as you drop back alongside him. Should he turn and face you, reposition yourself, and cue him again. This time, use the longe whip as an extension of your arm, bringing the whip deliberately toward his hocks, to encourage him to drive ahead, away from you.

Once you establish forward motion, don't be content with a half-circle before

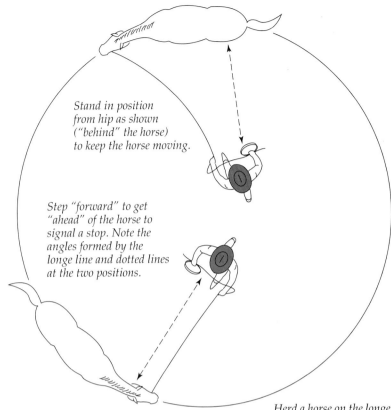

*Stand in position from hip as shown ("behind" the horse) to keep the horse moving.*

*Step "forward" to get "ahead" of the horse to signal a stop. Note the angles formed by the longe line and dotted lines at the two positions.*

Herd a horse on the longe line by stepping toward his hindquarters. Head him off by stepping ahead to stop him.

you say whoa. Move the horse around the circle several times, so that he understands to continue going forward, until you tell him otherwise. Should he try to cut off the circle, again use the whip as an extension of your arm, just as you would when leading him. When his body moves into the circle, toward you, point the whip toward the barrel of his body to create a barrier. Use the whip, as you used your thumb previously, to move the horse out of your territory.

When you're ready for the horse to stop, say whoa, and step ahead of his shoulder, bumping the line, if necessary, to reinforce the whoa command. He should stand quietly and await your next command. Should you walk toward the horse, reverse the whip, so that the less threatening handle, rather than the tail, points toward him. Take care in gathering the excess line as you go.

It requires practice to master longeing

*Longeing a horse on a line is a simple way to bring down his energy level or give him a few minutes to become accustomed to unfamiliar surroundings before saddling up.*

*Free-longeing a horse in a pen presents an excellent opportunity for you and your horse to learn one another's body language.*

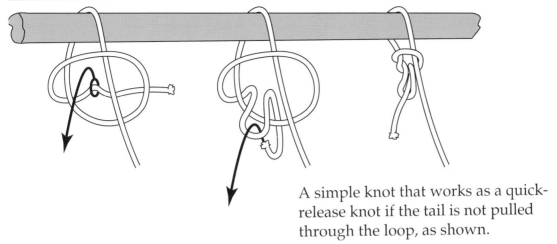

A simple knot that works as a quick-release knot if the tail is not pulled through the loop, as shown.

techniques. Above all, work safely. Take your time to ensure that you are handling the line safely, even stopping the horse, if necessary, to do so. Over time, you will be able to feed the line out, making a larger circle possible, or take in the line with ease. Eventually, you will be able to longe a horse at a walk, trot, and canter, making the circle larger or smaller as you work.

Make a point of working your horse in both directions, or on both sides, as horsemen describe it. Due to a horse's physical makeup, you must train his body to give the desired response to both the left-hand and the right-hand. You can't say, "Okay, you can do it to the left; now do the same thing going to the right." Horses don't work that way. Too, reversing direction periodically causes less fatigue and boredom for a horse.

## Tying Your Horse

A final consideration of ground work is knowing where to tie your horse, what to tie him to, and how to tie him safely.

When you choose a place to tie your horse, look for potential booby-traps. For example, don't tie your horse so near another horse that they can kick one another. That's inviting an accident. Check the area for anything that could injure or startle a horse. Make sure the ground is clear of loose wire, broken glass, and such. Check the fencing or barn wall for any

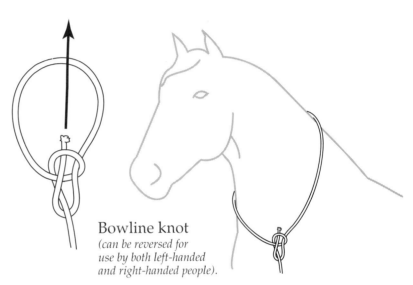

Bowline knot
*(can be reversed for use by both left-handed and right-handed people).*

exposed nails. In short, view the area with as critical an eye as you would use viewing a stall for rent.

Don't tie to or near a piece of equipment, such as a plow or tractor. A horse can get a leg or a halter hung, which can result in a lot of damage to both the animal and the equipment. Do not tie to anything the horse can move, such as a lawn chair, lawn mower, concrete block, dumpster, or even some horse trailers not hitched to a vehicle. Should a horse move the item, it could frighten him. Still tied, he might run with it, which makes the situation even scarier.

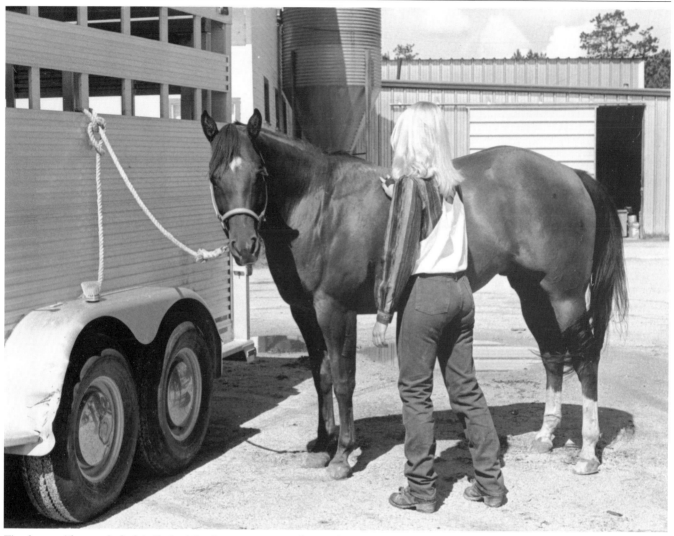

*Tie a horse with enough slack in the lead that he can move around somewhat and isn't forced to stand in one position. Be careful, however, not to tie him so long that he can get his legs entangled in the lead.*

Look overhead before you tie your horse. Check for potential hazards, such as a low-hanging limb or clothesline. Even an apparently uncluttered aisleway in the barn may be hazardous if your horse can knock bottles and items loose from a nearby shelf.

Tie your horse to something sturdy enough to hold him. Even a mature, broke horse can cause havoc, should a post be rotten at the ground and break with a slight tug. When tying to a fence, tie to the sturdier post, not to an easily broken board.

If you're uncertain about how high or low to tie a horse, the rule of thumb is to tie at the horse's eye level, or higher. If a horse tied low pulls back, this can result in a serious injury called a pulled-down neck.

You should allow enough slack in the lead so that your horse can shift his position from time to time. Be cautious, however, in allowing too much slack. If your horse can get his head down to the ground, he can probably get a front foot over the lead rope.

Two knots, in particular, find favor with horsemen. The accompanying illustrations show how to tie a quick-release knot and a bowline.

A quick-release is a simple slip knot; one snatch of the loose end, and a horse is free. Some horses, when they're tied, however, play with the end of the lead and inadvertently discover how to free themselves. To prevent this, drop the tail of the lead back through the knot's loop. Untying a horse will still be easy and convenient for you, but more difficult for the horse.

The bowline is more difficult to learn to tie, but useful in some situations. Should your halter break, you can tie a bowline around your horse's neck and still lead him to the barn. The bowline won't draw tighter or choke a horse. And, should a horse pull back when tied, a bowline often is easier to untie than other knots. Too, it's unlikely that a horse can untie a bowline by lipping the lead.

If you tie your horse regularly in the same spot, for grooming and saddling, you might want to permanently attach a lead with a quick-release snap there. Such snaps are easy to fasten to a halters, yet will release and open should a horse pull back hard against them. Trailer ties with quick-release snaps are also available commercially.

Be careful about using cross-ties, especially with young horses. Some horses panic when they find they can't move their head from side to side. Or, if they are suddenly startled, or object to something like clippers, they might strike with the front feet.

Pay particular attention when you tie your horse to a trailer. Don't tie to a low hitch or cross-brace, where your horse can get a foot over his lead. Check the position of the license plate especially, looking for sharp, exposed edges. If a tied horse can get a front foot over the edge of the plate, the resulting cut can be serious. Most trailer-tie loops are well-placed for the horse's safety, but not all are. Of necessity, some tie loops are placed near trailer windows and doors, so be sure those are secured before tying your horse.

# 11

# GROOMING YOUR HORSE

*Grooming, and even clipping, a horse can be a pleasant task, with the right approach.*

WITH PRACTICE, you'll soon be able to groom your horse quickly and thoroughly, giving him a cleaner hair coat and a shinier one. Regular grooming helps stimulate the skin pores, which creates more of the natural oils that put a sheen in a horse's coat. Grooming sessions also are a great way for you and your new horse to become better acquainted. Most horses relax when being groomed, so the experience can become a gentling process in which you accustom the horse to your touch. As an added benefit, you learn your horse's body—it's shape, texture, and feel—as it normally is. As a result, you notice when his body condition is not normal, and you can more quickly treat any cuts, scrapes, swelling, or soreness.

## Basic Grooming Tools

Good grooming doesn't require a lot of tools. Instead it results from using the available tools effectively and regularly. For ease of use, stash your supplies in a bucket or in a milk crate fastened to the barn wall. Some people like a cobbler's apron with pockets for grooming gear, and others purchase deep, two-sided trays from a discount store.

Here's what you might find in a basic grooming kit.

1/ *Currycomb.* A rubber or metal currycomb is used to loosen dried sweat or mud in the hair coat. A metal currycomb often breaks up heavy mud more easily than a rubber currycomb, but must be used with care on a horse's tender skin. A rubber currycomb, used in a circular motion, not only loosens and removes

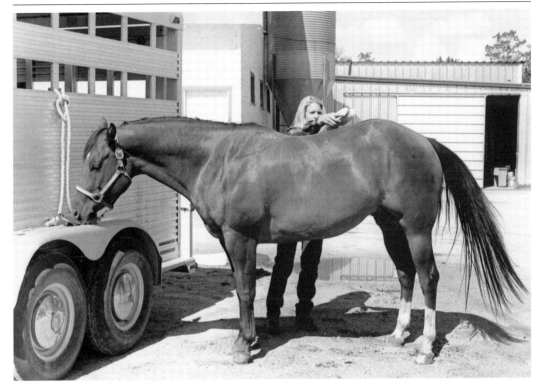

dried mud and sweat, but also has a massaging effect. However, never use a currycomb below the knees and hocks or on the head; those areas don't have enough flesh to cushion such a hard tool.

2/ *Coarse-bristled brush.* Often a rice-root or corn brush, this lifts away the dirt loosened by currying and can be used gently on the lower legs, mane, and tail. Use firm, short strokes with the brush to sweep the dirt away from the body, brushing with the lay of the hair. When grooming mane or tail hair, start at the bottom, moving up the length of the hair, working on a small section at the time.

3/ *Fine-bristled, soft brush.* A finishing-type brush, this is used to lift the finer particles of dirt missed by the coarser-bristled brush. Again, stroke with the lay of the hair, using short, brisk strokes.

4/ *Sponge or grooming cloth.* Dampen an old towel or a sponge to clean sweat marks on a horse's head, or to clean around his eyes and nostrils. A sponge or cloth can also be used to soften dried mud or manure on the bony lower legs.

5/ *Hoof pick.* It makes little difference whether you select a standard hoof pick or a collapsible pocket style. The important thing is to use a hoof pick to clean your horse's hoofs regularly. For more information, see the chapter on hoof care.

6/ *Mane and tail comb.* This wide-toothed comb is used to pick tangles from the mane or tail hair. Again, start from the bottom and work up, toward the roots. Use caution to prevent breaking the hair, and never try to pull out a tangle. Instead, work at it gently, untangling a little at the time.

7/ *Sweat scraper and/or shedding blade.* A sweat scraper has a dull edge and is used in a firm, sweeping motion to throw moisture off the hair coat, whether it's sweat or water from bathing a horse. Shedding blades, because they generally have a dull edge on one side, also can be used as a scraper to shed water. The small teeth on the other side of a shedding blade facilitate removal of winter hair and dried mud.

## The Grooming Routine

Some horsemen groom from head to tail; others groom the body first and then the head. One horseman may clean his horse's feet after grooming, while another does so beforehand. After grooming your horse several times, you will find a procedure that's comfortable for you. The following describes the steps in grooming your horse; you can arrange the steps in whatever order you prefer.

1/ *Grooming the horse's body.* Many people begin with a rubber curry in the

**Regularly cleaning your horse's feet allows you to familiarize yourself with a normal, healthy foot so you can better recognize when a foot problem is developing.**

93

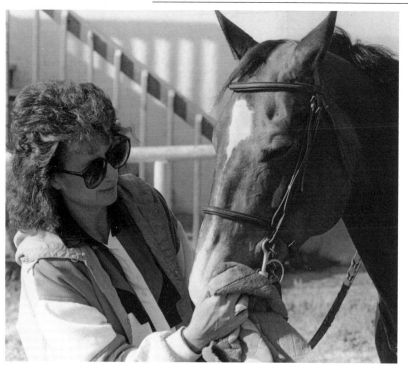

*A soft towel works well for grooming a horse's face, particularly around the eyes or nostrils.*

right hand and a body brush in the left. Other people prefer a two-step procedure, currying a horse first and then brushing him. Horsemen generally groom the near side of a horse first, then move around to the off side.

Begin working on the neck, right behind his ears. Clean down the neck to the chest and between the front legs. Groom from the upper neck back, toward the withers. As you groom the shoulder, continue down the horse's foreleg until you reach the knee.

Then move up to the withers, grooming the back, his barrel, and underneath his belly. Use caution in grooming his belly; a startled horse sometimes cow-kicks, reaching under his belly with a hind foot and swinging it to the side. Pay particular attention to the cinch area, cleaning it well to help prevent cinch sores. Remember, too, that horses often are ticklish in their flanks, so use a firm stroke, rather than a light one. Moving up to the loin area, groom the rump and hind leg, down to the hock.

Once the near side is clean, move to the far side of your horse and follow the same procedure. When the horse has been curried and brushed, use a finishing brush to whisk away the scurf and fine particles you might have missed earlier. Again, begin on the near side, working from the neck back, and to the hock.

2/ *Grooming the head.* Use several light brush strokes to clean a horse's head, rather than a few hard strokes. There's little padding between the skin and bone there, and harsh strokes can be uncomfortable for the horse. If necessary, dampen your sponge or grooming cloth and use it to clean his head, especially around the eyes and nostrils.

3/ *Grooming the lower legs.* Groom the lower leg in much the same manner as the head, working gently from the knees and hocks down to the hoofs. If dried mud or manure is a problem, use a damp sponge or cloth, or water from a hose, to soften it and wash it away.

4/ *Grooming the mane and tail.* Generally, horses are not as touchy about having their manes and tails groomed as some tender-headed people are when having their hair styled. Horse hair can break easily although a horse may give no indication that you have pulled too hard. Again, work from the bottom up, toward the roots, untangling small portions of hair, one at the time.

When you groom the tail, don't stand directly behind a horse, in his blind spot. Instead, stand a little to one side, where he can comfortably keep his eye on you. If he does kick, he is less likely to hit you.

5/ *Cleaning his feet.* This is one of the best preventive measures you can take to ensure that you have a sound horse to ride. Regularly cleaning your horse's feet allows you to familiarize yourself with a normal, healthy foot so you can better recognize when a foot problem is developing. The chapter on hoof care gives more detailed information about trimming, shoeing, and such.

Use caution in cleaning your horse's feet. Work from the near foreleg to the near hind leg, then from the off hind leg to the off foreleg. Since he is a creature of habit, your horse will become more comfortable, more quickly, with the cleaning procedure when a routine is used.

*Stand on the near side, facing the horse's hindquarters. Put your left hand at his shoulder. Bend over and slide your right hand down the front cannon, until your hand is a little above the fetlock. Use your left hand to push the horse's weight onto his right foreleg. When he relaxes and shifts his weight, pick up his foot with your right hand.*

*When the foot is up, you can bring it between your knees, tightening your legs around his leg, to help hold the foot in position for cleaning.*

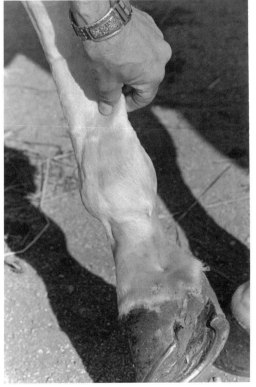

*Or, you can rest his foot across your left thigh as you clean out the foot.*

*If your horse seems unresponsive when you try to pick up his foot, try squeezing at the back of the lower leg or tapping it gently with the hoof pick.*

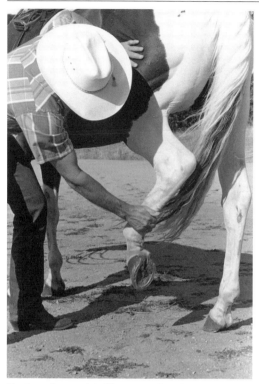 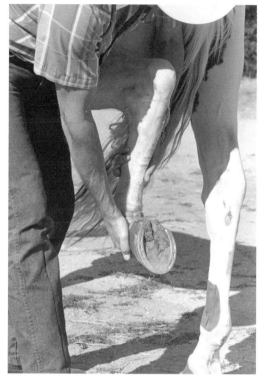

*To clean the near hind leg, again face the rear, standing close to your horse's body. Use your left hand to rub from his loin down his rump, until your hand is at his hip, where you can more easily push his weight to the off side. As with the foreleg, firmly move your right hand down the hind leg, to about the middle of the cannon. As you push against the horse's hip with your left hand, pick up the lower leg with your right when he shifts his weight over, to the off side. Bend the leg at the hock, but do not pull it out to the side. His hind leg can easily swing forward or back, but pulling it to the side is uncomfortable, and your horse could show resistance.*

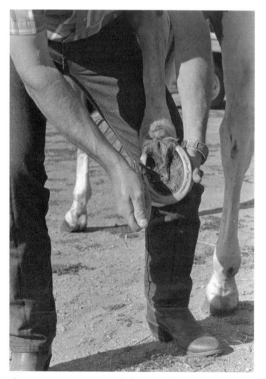 

*As you step more toward the rear of your horse, stay near his body, keeping his leg close to your left leg. As his leg rotates from under his belly out behind him, place the leg across your thigh, to support it while you clean the foot, or you can support his leg between your legs.*

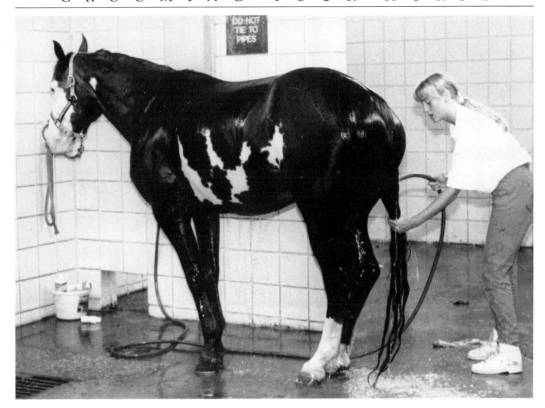

*Many horsemen simply rinse a horse with clear water following a hard workout, to remove the sweat. Whenever shampoo is used, it's important to rinse a horse's hair coat thoroughly.*

Hold the hoof pick with the point facing away from you and braced against the heel of your hand. Loosen debris in the foot with the point of the pick, by working from the heel toward the toe. The frog, in the center of his foot, is somewhat triangular in shape. Clean around the frog thoroughly. Those crevices are where infections, such as thrush, can flourish. Visually inspect the foot, too, for any injuries, and check for loose shoes.

Should your horse's hoofs be dry and brittle, this is also a good time to use hoof-dressing. There are many commercial preparations on the market, or your veterinarian or farrier can recommend one.

The series of photographs shows how to pick up a near front foot and a near hind foot. Reverse the procedure when working on the right side of the horse.

## Washing Your Horse

Sooner or later, most horsemen wash, or at least hose off, their horses. People often hose their horses with clear water, to remove heavy sweat or caked-in mud. They might well do so several times a week in warmer climates. The clear water, however, is not harsh on a horse's hair coat and doesn't strip it of the natural oils.

Washing a horse with harsh shampoo, however, can strip the natural oils from a horse's coat, so use only a mild shampoo if you find it necessary to wash a horse. Commercial products, formulated especially for horses, are available and have complete instructions.

The first step is to rinse the horse with water, wetting his coat completely. Some people prefer to mix a small amount of shampoo with water in a bucket; others prefer to squirt the shampoo onto a sponge or brush, which is then applied to the wet horse. Work the lather through the horse's coat, moving from the front of the horse back.

More important than the shampooing of a horse is the final rinsing. The shampoo should be hosed thoroughly from your horse's hair. Not only could the residue dull his coat, it can be itchy, and he could wind up with a skin rash as well.

*Scraping excess water from the hair coat helps speed the drying process.*

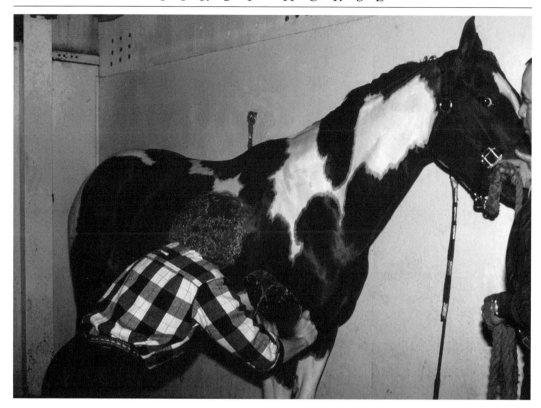

After rinsing completely, use a sweat scraper to remove excess water from the hair coat. As with the daily grooming routine, work from the neck back, on the near side, then the off side. Use brisk strokes, moving with the hair, to sling the water away from the horse. A sweat scraper, too, is like a curry comb, in that it is far too harsh to be used on the bonier parts of the horse's legs and head.

Use judgment in deciding when and where to wash your horse. Some barns have wash racks indoors, out of the wind, with both hot and cold water available. Such an arrangement makes washing a horse possible even in inclement weather. If you must wash your horse outside, take the weather into consideration. Horses can become chilled, just as people do, when they are wet and in the wind. Too, the wind can make it more difficult for you to stay dry when using the hose.

Consider, too, where you plan to wash your horse and walk or tie him to dry. Be sure you are not hosing him on a surface that becomes slick when wet. That can be dangerous.

If you're certain that your horse is hose-broke, it's okay to tie him when you wash him. Don't tie him if you aren't certain he can tolerate being sprayed with water. Be considerate of others, too, when you do tie your horse to wash him. Don't inadvertently spray water on tack and gear or other riders. Be cautious about tying your horse in direct sunlight to dry. Some coat colors tend to fade with prolonged exposure to the sun.

If you're not certain about how your horse will respond to being hosed with water, use caution in your approach. It's best not to tie the horse in this case. Although you could handle the lead with one hand, and the hose with the other, it's best if you have a friend hold your horse while you introduce him to the water hose. If your first horse is a mature, broke one, it's likely he is hose-broke. But, again, until you are certain that's the case, it's better to have assistance.

To accustom a horse to being hosed, use a soft spray of water, aimed toward the ground, as you approach him from a distance. Use much the same gradual

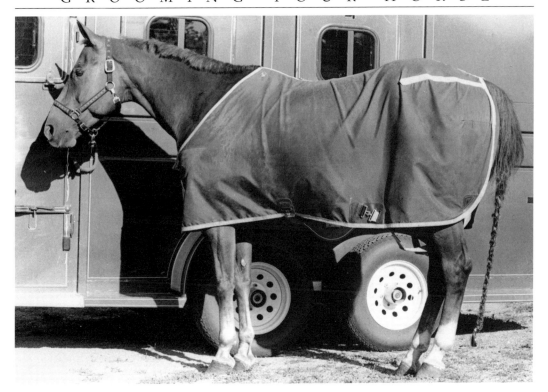

*Here's a horse blanketed. Such gear is available in many weights and materials, with the heavier blankets suitable for cold or rainy weather, while the lightweight sheets serve more to protect a horse's hair coat from dust and sunshine. The sun can bleach a coat. The braid helps keep the tail clean and free from tangles, and prevents tail hairs from being broken off.*

approach as described in chapter 9, where a horse becomes accustomed to a slicker.

As the horse shows signs of relaxing, gradually move closer with the hose. When you are near enough, begin gently running the water over the horse's lower legs. Over a period of time, direct the water up his legs, toward his body. As with grooming, direct the water on the horse from front to back, beginning with the neck. Not every horse will accept a spray of water directed into his face, nor do horses like getting water in their ears. So approach washing the head with care. You may find washing his face with a damp sponge a better alternative.

## Beyond the Basics

Grooming horses for show is a more involved process, with the greatest of attention shown to every minor detail. Not only are coats, manes, and tails shampooed, they are conditioned as well. Hoof polishes, rather than dressings, are often used. Manes and tails are sometimes pulled or thinned, and tails are braided and bagged. Manes, too, can be braided or even banded. A mane-tamer, an oversized hairnet, is sometimes fastened around the neck to help ensure that the mane hair lies flat and in one direction.

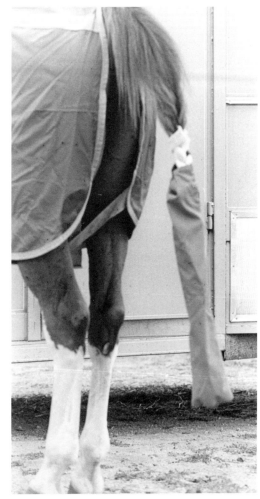

*Tails are often bagged to keep them looking their best. The bag is secured by ties that are woven into the braid.*

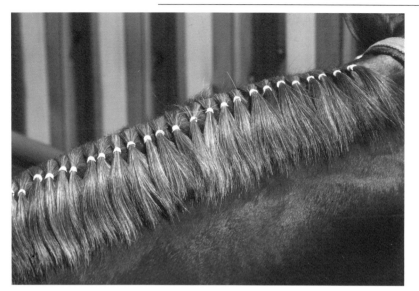

*In recent years, banding a mane, after it has been shortened, has been popular in the show arena.*

For detailed and illustrated how-to techniques for western show grooming, see the *Western Horseman* booklet, *Grooming*. It gives complete information about clipping, bathing, mane and tail care, and show preparation.

Many horsemen, who don't show, usually clip only a bridle path and the fetlock hair on their horses' lower legs.

A bridle path is exactly as described. A path, where the crown piece of the bridle rests, is cut through the mane and usually is just a few inches in length. The rule of thumb for the length of the bridle path: Lay your horse's ear back, alongside his neck, and take note of where the end of the ear lies. That point is the end of the bridle path; it begins at the point of a horse's poll.

Some horses, such as draft horses, have heavier hair growth on the legs and seldom are trimmed there. Trimming the hair on the lower leg, however, gives a neater and cleaner appearance on most horses.

Although it's easy to clip a horse's leg, it's possible you will create a streaked appearance. But with practice, most people can learn to clip smoothly and evenly. Generally, clippers are run down the horse's leg with the lay of the hair, using light and even strokes. Don't worry if you streak the hair; a week or so later, it won't be that noticeable.

If you're not sure that your horse will accept being clipped, seek help from a knowledgeable person.

When approached correctly, many horses who are frightened by clippers can become desensitized to the noise as time goes by. But the problem must be approached carefully and thoughtfully. When mishandled, this situation only compounds the problem of clipping a horse.

If you must, at first, hire an experienced professional to help you clip the first few times. The dividends may be well worth it if they result in your being able to handle the chore yourself. Although some horses may never become totally accepting of clippers, many become better, or even nonchalant, about being clipped.

Clippers come in a variety of styles and sizes; some are even battery-operated. Some models offer a lever adjustment, to

Clipping plays a major role in grooming for shows. Clipping styles vary from one breed to another, and even from one event to another. The hair on almost any body part of a horse is fair game when people prepare to show their horses—fetlocks, coronet bands, muzzle, ears, jawline, and even long eye-hairs.

Remember that nature gave the horse hair for a reason. Ear hair, for example, helps protect the ears from insects, and the hair on his muzzle is akin to feelers, helping him to be more aware of his surroundings.

In some cases, a horse's entire body is often clipped in the show season, to eliminate the longer winter hair growth, or to freshen a sun-faded coat. However, such clipped horses often must be stabled and blanketed during inclement weather, since their natural protection from the elements has been removed.

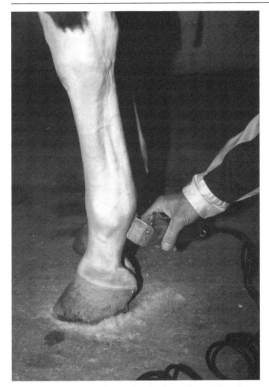

*Although the entire lower leg is often clipped for show, many people trim only the long hair on the fetlock.*

*This horse has been clipped for showing, including the hair on the inside of the ears, but many horsemen are satisfied to trim only a bridle-path, leaving hair on the ears and muzzle alone. Hair in the ears protects them from flies and other insects.*

set the closeness of the cutting blade, from a coarse cut to an extremely short one. Other clippers have removable blades, so you can determine the depth of the cut by changing the blade.

One thing to consider when you select a pair of clippers, is how noisy they are. The quieter the clippers run, the easier it will be for your horse to accept them.

The clipper blades can be sharpened repeatedly, and many companies offer a sharpening service for their products. Or call a local beautician or barber to find out who sharpens their clipper blades.

Two things are important to remember in using clippers. 1/ The cleaner your horse's hair is when you start clipping, the less wear and tear on the clipper blades. 2/ Your clippers will last longer when you perform the routine maintenance, such as oiling, recommended in the instruction manual.

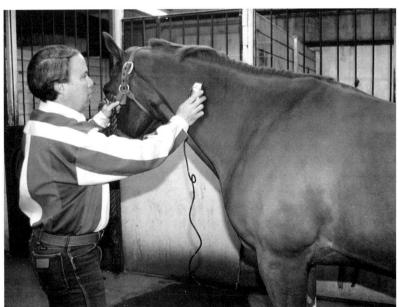

*When using clippers, approach a horse gradually, allowing him time to become accustomed to the sound and vibration.*

101

# SADDLING UP

## 12

*Be sure the blanket is clean underneath, where it rests next to a horse's back.*

AFTER GROOMING your horse, you're ready to saddle up and use your new gear. Saddling and bridling your horse may seem awkward to you at first. Once you've done it a few times, however, and learned to adjust your gear properly, saddling isn't that difficult.

Many people tie their horses to saddle them. When your horse is tied, you will need to move from side to side while saddling. Do so carefully by walking a safe distance behind him. Don't step under a tied lead, between the horse and a wall or fence. Remember, his vision isn't good under his head, so it isn't a safe place for you to be.

Other horsemen prefer to hold the lead in the left hand while they saddle, to allow for more control of the horse. If you hold the lead, rather than tie your horse, you can move from side to side at the front. You can control the horse's head, as necessary, and you won't have to duck out of his field of vision as you move.

## The Blanket, Saddle, and Breast Collar

It's a good idea to have both the blanket and saddle nearby, before you start to saddle. Should you put the blanket or pad on a horse and then return to the barn or trailer for your saddle, the blanket may slide from his back before you return. This sometimes happens when a horse shifts his weight around. So the closer at hand the saddle is, the better.

First, turn your blanket over, checking underneath for twigs or burrs that could

102

cause a sore spot on your horse's back. If your blanket falls to the ground while you're getting the saddle, check underneath it again.

Place the blanket on the horse's back, a little forward of where it should be, and slide it back into position over the withers. This ensures that the hair lies smoothly under the blanket. Check to see if the blanket is hanging evenly on both sides of the horse, and smooth any wrinkles you might find.

Pick up the saddle, by the horn, with your right hand. With your left hand, sweep the off-side stirrup, cinches, and saddle strings to the right, laying them over the saddle. If the fender and stirrup won't stay, hook the right stirrup over the horn to keep it out of the way when you position the saddle on the horse.

If you don't immobilize the off-side gear, it could startle the horse as you swing the saddle onto his back. Too, a hard cinch ring, flying through the air, can bruise a horse's leg. A little flying gear and a few bruises later, your horse will have learned to dodge when you try to saddle him.

One person may find it easier to put the right hand around the horn, with the fingers tucked behind it, and swing the saddle up and over the horse's back. Another person may not physically be able to lift and position a saddle with one hand. If that's the case, place the left hand at the front of the saddle, near the gullet, and the right hand on the cantle at the rear, and lift the saddle onto the horse. Use the method that works best for you.

At the peak of your lift, the saddle should be high enough to clear the withers. But don't turn the saddle loose, letting it flop on the horse's back. This makes a horse flinchy when being saddled. Maintain control instead, holding the saddle steady as you settle it into place.

Step around to the right and release the off-side gear, making sure that the cinch isn't twisted and that the blanket is straight. Returning to the near side, hook the left stirrup over the horn, to keep it out of the way while you cinch up.

The following is not a guideline; it is an important rule of safety: Always fasten the more snug-fitting front cinch first, on a double-rigged saddle, and then the rear cinch. Always unfasten the rear cinch first, before releasing the tighter front cinch. To do otherwise invites trouble.

For example, if only the back cinch is fastened and the horse spooks, the saddle is apt to slip sideways and end up under the belly, scaring the horse even more. The result is usually a wrecked saddle and possibly an injured horse.

Use caution when reaching under the horse for the front cinch, maintaining a close watch on him. If you are the least bit uneasy about reaching for the cinch, make a loop in the latigo, doubling it, and use the loop as an extension of your arm. Reach under the horse and bring the loop up to encircle the cinch so you can pull the cinch toward the near side. The more familiar you become with your horse, the more comfortable reaching for the cinch will become.

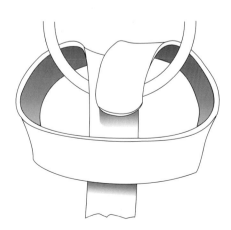

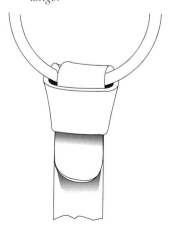

*If your cinch doesn't have a buckle, a cinch knot can be used to fasten the latigo.*

*Place the blanket a little forward on the withers to ensure that the hair is smoothed back, rather than ruffled forward, as saddling continues.*

*Flip the offside gear over the seat before saddling up to ensure that a dangling cinch buckle doesn't strike the horse's leg.*

Run the long latigo through the cinch ring. Then bring the latigo up, putting it over and through the ring in the rigging, and then down and back through the cinch ring. Pull the latigo so the cinch is snug. Use slow, steady pressure, and buckle the cinch tongue through a hole in the latigo. Run your fingers under the latigo, above the buckle, pulling toward yourself to snug the tongue against the latigo. If your cinch doesn't buckle, see the illustration to learn how to tie a cinch knot. Place the excess latigo in the keeper on the near side of your saddle.

Check that the cinch is centered from one side to the other. If the near-side cinch ring almost meets the rigging ring, loosen the latigo, move to the off-side, and take up the billet there. Most cinches have a D-ring in the center of them, so use it to gauge how well-balanced your cinch adjustment is.

Many horses have a tendency to "blow up," as it's called, when first being cinched. When they let their air out, the cinch is far looser than it originally seemed. So give a horse a minute or two, after the initial cinching, and tighten the cinch again. One rule of thumb states that, when your cinch is properly tightened, you should be able to get your fingers, held flat against the horse, between the

*Allow a few inches clearance when swinging a saddle over a horse's back to ensure that the blanket isn't knocked askew.*

*Ease the saddle onto the horse's back, letting it settle there gently.*

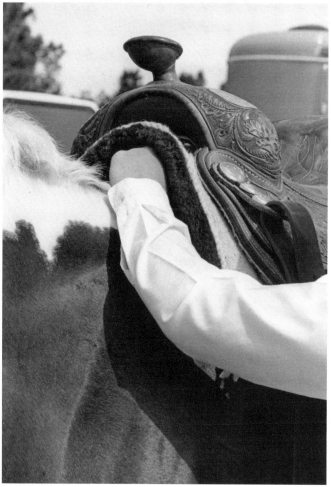

*Lift the blanket well into the gullet of the saddle to help prevent it from pulling against the withers, once the saddle is cinched.*

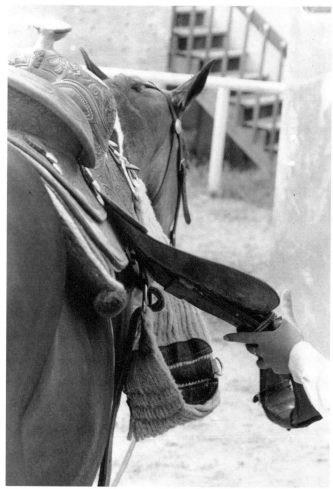

*Lower the offside gear easily, so that it doesn't slap a horse in the side and startle him.*

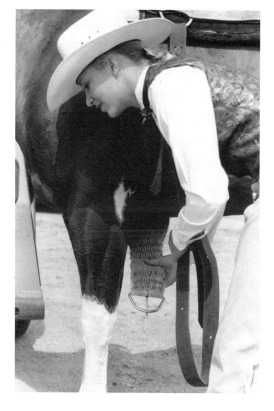

*Face forward when reaching under a horse's belly for the cinch. You're less likely to take a blow to your head, should a horse kick.*

cinch and your horse's side.

Fasten your back cinch next. The rear cinch is adjusted more loosely than the front one and hangs just about an inch below a horse's belly. If there's too much slack in the rear cinch, a horse can get a hind foot between it and his belly, when he kicks at a fly or when he's crossing water (when he picks his feet up extra high). It's also possible to snag a limb (from down timber) or brush in a too-loose back cinch when in rough country.

Buckle your breast collar, making sure it fits over the points of the horse's shoulders. However, a breast collar shouldn't be so snug, where his neck joins his chest, that it cuts off a horse's air. Finally, fasten the center piece between his front legs to the D-ring in the center of the front cinch.

## Unsaddling

When you unsaddle, do the entire process in reverse. First unfasten the breast

*Wrap the latigo smoothly, running your fingers under it to ensure that the wraps aren't pinching a horse's skin.*

*Be careful not to cinch a horse too tightly. Once the buckle tongue has been inserted in the latigo, pull the outside wrap against the tongue to "lock it" and ensure that the buckle stays fastened.*

collar from the cinch D-ring. Then unbuckle the near side of the breast collar. To keep your gear from dragging on the ground, go to the far side of your horse and rebuckle the strap you just unfastened. Hang that loop over your saddle horn.

Unfasten the rear cinch first, before you loosen the front cinch. This is important, for safety's sake. Finally, unbuckle the front cinch. Walk to the off side and buckle both front and rear cinches through the carrier, to keep them off the ground. Or use a front saddle string to tie the cinches up.

Before you pull the saddle off your horse, grasp it by the horn and give a little shake to let the air circulate underneath. The, lift the saddle as you take it off; don't drag it off.

# The Bridle

It is acceptable to place the bridle over your horse's halter. If you do, you can unfasten the lead and tie it to the saddle for easy access, or tie the tail of it to your horn.

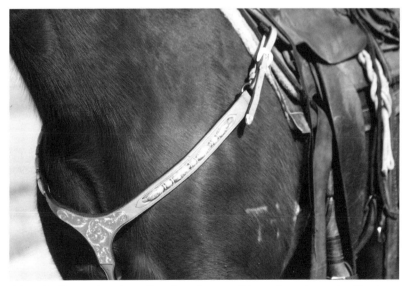

*A breast collar can be a decorative piece of gear, as this one is, and a serviceable piece of equipment as well.*

*This series demonstrates how to buckle the halter around the neck and then bridle the horse.*

*Use the thumb of your left hand in the interdental space to help open the mouth.*

*Handle the ears gently (left) when pulling the crownpiece of the bridle over them. Be sure to fasten the throatlatch.*

Many people, however, prefer to drop the halter entirely before bridling. They usually unfasten the crownpiece of the halter and refasten it around the neck until the bridle is in place. Then, should something unexpected happen while bridling, the horse is less apt to get loose. Other people sometimes wrap the reins around a horse's neck and hold them throughout the bridling process. This keeps your reins out of the dirt as well. Do whatever best suits you.

Stand close to your horse to bridle him, just behind his head on the near side. This position makes it less likely for the horse to hit you in the face if he slings his head. Rest your right hand at the top of his neck, over his poll. Move this hand between the ears and down the head until you can grasp the crown of the bridle with your right hand. Don't be timid in your actions; be firm and sure.

**If a horse resists opening his mouth, with your left hand still on the bit, slide your left thumb between his lips. Press down with your thumb on the interdental space to open his mouth.**

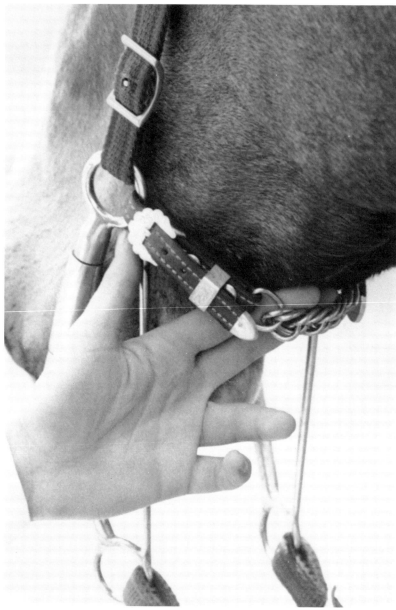

*The rule of thumb calls for enough slack in the curb chain that two fingers can be placed comfortably between it and the horse's jaw.*

As you lift the bridle onto the horse's head with the right hand, drop your left down to grasp the bit, using the first two fingers under the mouthpiece and the last two on the curb strap, to spread it and the bit apart. This leaves your left thumb free, if necessary, to apply pressure to the toothless interdental space on the lower jaw, should your horse resist the bit. Before you bridle a horse the first time, it's a good idea to part his lips on the left side and locate the interdental space.

Don't be too forceful with your right hand; ease the bridle up the horse's head until the mouthpiece of the bit rests against his mouth. As he opens his mouth, pull the bridle up with your right hand, gently sliding the bit between his teeth. If a horse resists opening his mouth, with your left hand still on the bit, slide your left thumb between his lips. Press down with your thumb on the interdental space to open his mouth. Don't bang the bit against a horse's mouth if he is uncooperative; that only adds to the problem, making him even more resistant to opening his mouth.

Once the bit is in his mouth, bring the crownpiece of the headstall over the ears, gently but firmly. His ears are supple enough to lie flat against his neck as the headstall is positioned, and will pop back up between the crown and the browband. If you are using a one-ear bridle, cup your hand around the base of his right ear and bring it through the earpiece. Use a smooth upward motion.

Buckle the throatlatch, but not so tightly that it will choke a horse when he flexes at the poll, bringing his head into a more vertical position.

Notice where the bit rests in relation to the corner of the horse's mouth, where the lips join. The old rule of thumb was to adjust a headstall just tight enough to form a slight wrinkle in the corner of a horse's mouth. Nowadays, however, horsemen sometimes leave the adjustment looser, allowing a horse more leeway to learn to "pack a bit," or carry it more comfortably in his mouth. Use the buckles on the cheekpieces of the bridle to make this adjustment.

Follow the two-finger rule of thumb to adjust the curb strap. It should be loose enough than you can insert two fingers between the strap and your horse's head. This gives a horse relief from pressure on the bit until you apply pressure by using your hands on the reins.

Once you have made the necessary adjustments to the bridle, be sure to fasten the ends of the straps through the buckle keepers. The fewer things that flop against a horse's head, the better.

# Removing the Bridle

To remove a bridle, fasten the halter around the horse's neck as you did before. Unfasten the throatlatch on the bridle. With your right hand on the crownpiece, smoothly bring the bridle forward, over the horse's ears. Once the bridle is over his ears, pause briefly. Sometimes it takes a horse a second or two to realize that now is the time to open his mouth and release the bit. If that's the case, be patient and let the horse drop the bit, rather than forcefully pulling it from his mouth.

# A Final Check

Now that you can saddle up and adjust your gear, it's time to ride. But before mounting up, it's a good idea to untrack your horse and check the cinch one more time. So lead your horse up a few steps, and tighten the cinch again, if necessary. If it is, untrack him again before you mount. Although it isn't common, a horse occasionally will rear and come over backwards if he isn't untracked before mounting.

Give a final, close look at both bridle and saddle. Fix anything that isn't as it should be. Checking your equipment regularly is one of the best things you can do to ensure your safety. Now you're ready to ride.

# LET'S RIDE

**13**

AT LAST—your first horse is home, and you're saddled up and ready to ride. It's time to give some thought to horsemanship. That's the art of handling or managing a horse, and the term applies whether you're afoot or astride your horse. This chapter, however, discusses the principles of good horsemanship as they apply to riding.

The principles, simply put, are guidelines that help you ride as one with your horse. These guidelines have not been set arbitrarily. Mankind has been riding horses for hundreds of years, and the principles of horsemanship have resulted from this collective experience. And, yes, there are always exceptions to every rule and other ways of doing things. But these guidelines have well-served most of the people riding most of the horses most of the time. So that's a pretty good place to start increasing the odds that you'll become an accomplished rider.

## Mounting and Dismounting

Effective horsemanship focuses on control of the horse—even when you're mounting and dismounting.

The adjustment of the reins in your left hand, as you mount or dismount, is important; these are your brakes, should your horse step out before you are properly positioned. Take up the reins short enough that, by moving your left hand a few inches, you have contact with the horse's mouth. You can say whoa, pull back, and stop any forward motion if necessary. On the other hand, don't adjust the reins so tightly that

*Once you're mounted and riding, the time, money, and effort used in maintaining a horse seem mighty worthwhile.*

the horse starts backing to avoid the continuous pressure on his mouth.

To mount, place the left hand, with the reins in it, on the horse's neck, just ahead of the withers. Once you have placed your left foot in the stirrup, your right hand moves to the horn.

You can position your body in one of two ways to mount. Either is acceptable.

1/ This method is good for mounting green, or unschooled, horses who are less apt to stand quietly, or for mounting a strange horse when you are uncertain of his response. Should the horse move forward as you mount, the motion will carry you into the saddle that much faster.

Standing at your horse's left shoulder, make about a quarter-turn with your body to face more toward the horse's rump. Don't, however, lock your head into this position; use it to keep an eye on both the front and the rear end of the horse.

With your right hand, twist the left stirrup around, placing the ball of your left foot in it. As you reach for the horn with your right hand and mount up, use your left knee against the horse's body to help prevent poking his side with the toe of your boot.

Don't stand flat-footed when you mount up. Instead, keep your weight balanced on the ball of your right foot, ready to bounce up and off the ground. To swing onto the horse, push yourself off the ground with your foot, rather than pulling yourself up by the arms. This only pulls your saddle off-center.

2/ The second method of mounting is much the same as the first. The difference? You stand facing more to the front. With the reins in your left hand and on the horse's neck, place your left foot in the stirrup, again taking care not to bump the horse in the side. Grab hold of the horn with your right hand. With a bounce of the right foot, push off the ground, and swing into the saddle.

A short person must use caution when using this method to mount. Sometimes, in order to reach the stirrup, his body position can shift farther back, alongside the horse's body, which leaves the person more at risk for getting kicked.

No matter which method you use, as your right leg swings over the horse, settle your body gently into the saddle. Don't slam into it; that only causes a horse to flinch as you mount, anticipating a blow to his back. Once you're astride the horse,

promptly place your right foot in the off-side stirrup.

The dismount is much the same as the mount, but in reverse. Again, be sure the reins are well-adjusted in your left hand so that you can maintain control. With your left hand on the horse's neck and your right on the horn, swing your right leg over the cantle of the saddle. Your left foot rests lightly in the stirrup.

Don't swing out, away from the horse. Keep your body in, close to the horse, well-centered over him. This makes it easier for both you and the horse to stay balanced. As your right foot drops to the ground, shift your weight to the right foot, and let your left foot slide from the stirrup.

Some youngsters' legs are too short for them to keep the right foot on the ground while maintaining the left foot's position in the stirrup. This can place a child somewhat at risk for getting hung in the stirrup. In this case, it is better for a child to swing the right foot over to dismount, slide his left foot from the stirrup, and drop to the ground, landing on both feet.

*Although not the method taught in a horsemanship class, putting a knee in the stirrup to climb aboard works well for many youngsters. Others sometimes lead their mounts alongside a fence, or trailer to mount, but horses often learn to step away, just far enough that mounting is difficult, if not impossible.*

*When adjusting stirrup
length, use the old rule of
thumb that calls for the
bottom of the stirrup to
strike the ankle bone.*

However, this can also create another problem if there isn't enough slack in the reins. A smaller child using a properly adjusted rein, as he drops to the ground, can unintentionally pull the horse to the left, which increases the chances of getting stepped on. The safest alternative: Someone else should hold the horse and let the child concentrate on clearing the saddle as he dismounts.

## Assume the Position

Good horsemanship requires a proper position in the saddle, and that's not possible without properly adjusting the stirrup length first.

An old rule of thumb: Drop your foot from the stirrup. The ankle bone should, approximately, strike the stirrup tread. This should put you about 3 inches above the saddle seat when you stand in the stirrups, which is another rule of thumb. These, however, are only guidelines. Too short a

stirrup length, although feeling more secure, forces the legs too far forward, and too long a stirrup causes the rider's legs to drop back. Either way, a rider's legs are out from under his center of balance.

Too, a horse's conformation can affect stirrup length somewhat, as can the type of riding you pursue. Riding the same length stirrup on a wide horse feels shorter than it does when riding a horse of slighter build. The faster-paced your riding activity, the more comfortable you'll probably be with a slightly shorter stirrup length. A barrel racer or reiner, for example, usually feels more secure with a shorter stirrup length than would be used by a pleasure rider.

When you ride, think of yourself as a puppet with a string that runs from the top of your head, down through your ears, shoulders, and hips, and to the backs of your heels. This is the best position for a balanced ride. When you feel as if things have gone awry and you have "lost your seat" in the saddle, mentally pull the string. As you do, your physical position changes, coming into better alignment.

Ideally, you sit squarely in the saddle, eyes facing forward, not down. If you look at the ground continually, your upper body will follow your eyes downward and won't be in proper alignment. Your shoulders should be even; the rein-hand's shoulder position shouldn't "lead" the other one. The elbows are quiet, carried close to the torso.

Your hips should be as square as your shoulders. A good horseman rides more on his crotch, rather than the buttocks, to maximize the use of his legs. The lower back should be relaxed and soft so that the pelvis can roll easily with a horse's motion. The knees also remain soft, not locked stiffly into place, and should lie quietly along the cinch line. Generally, the toes turn slightly outward, with the heels pressed down, lower than the toes.

When you ride, your entire body gives signals to the horse, not just your hands, feet, or voice. For example, when cueing a horse to move out, your upper body tends to lean forward, urging him on. When stopping a horse, you tend to lean back as you say whoa. Such cues from your body result, sometimes, not so much from conscious thought as from your inner guidance system seeking to maintain its balance. Rather than fighting such motion, relax and move with it, letting your bal-

ance system take control. You will "find the middle of the saddle," as horsemen describe it, that much quicker.

The movement of the upper body over the motion of the horse, however, does not release a rider from the constraints of good horsemanship. Good body alignment, as previously described, with the heels down, holds true no matter what the gait. As a horse travels faster, the rider's body moves somewhat more forward in the saddle to compensate for the increased speed, but the basic body position doesn't change.

When you are riding, periodically check your body position. If you find, for example, that your toes drop down, your feet fall back, and your body curls over the horn as you increase the speed of your horse's gait, slow down and pull the puppet string. Realign your body position before continuing at a faster gait. For safety's sake, it's best not to try for too much speed until you can maintain a good seat in the saddle. Don't get discouraged; maintaining correct body position will become a subconscious habit faster than you think.

# Building Confidence

Take a few minutes to get comfortable in the saddle. Stand up in your stirrups, then melt softly down into the saddle. Keep your lower legs as still and quiet as possible when you do. Using your upper legs and torso, lift yourself from the saddle, rather than pushing yourself up by the toes, which leaves your heels up and improperly positioned.

A key to good horsemanship is maintaining a soft, supple body. You can't do that if you're apprehensive and tense, so wiggle around in your saddle a bit at first, bending and twisting, then moving back into proper position. It will help you feel more at ease because you can control the various positions you take and can practice balancing yourself in the saddle.

It's also good to "drop" the stirrups, or take your feet from them, a few times and then find your stirrups, reinserting your feet. Sooner or later, everyone loses or

*To improve your balance and your confidence have a friend longe the horse while you try some exercises in the saddle.*

**When you start riding, the more consistent your cues are, the faster and more consistently a horse learns to give the desired response.**

"blows" a stirrup, so prepare yourself. When it happens, you'll make a comfortable recovery.

If you feel it necessary, have someone hold the horse while you find your seat in the saddle. Better yet, mount up and have an experienced horseman longe your horse while you practice a few suppling exercises at a walk and trot, or even a canter. You can, for example, extend both arms to the side while being longed, or alternately swing them forward and back, to help build confidence in your balance.

Upper body control is important to riding well and can be enhanced by raising up in the saddle, making sure the lower legs and feet are properly positioned for stability. After standing up a few moments, softly sit back in the saddle without displacing your lower legs. Hold the horn at first, if you need it, to maintain your balance. Later, try standing for a few strides at a walk or a trot. You'll probably get a little sore when you first practice, but you'll be building the body control to become a well-balanced rider.

## Holding the Reins

By correctly holding the reins, you maximize the effectiveness of your hand signals to the horse, whether you're holding the reins in one hand or two.

Many right-handed people learn to ride using the left hand on the reins. This leaves the right free for roping, opening gates, and such, and vice-versa for left-handed riders. It's a good practice to follow.

There are two methods of holding the reins with one hand. The method used depends on the type reins on the bridle. Split reins are held in one manner, and reins with a romal are held in another.

1/ To properly position the hand when using split reins, point your index finger and rotate your hand so that the knuckles are up, on a horizontal plane. Drop your index finger between the reins. Close the other three fingers around the reins from one side and the thumb from the other.

Remember when riding to keep your knuckles up. If you roll your hand to the side, it will shorten the rein between your index finger and thumb an inch or so, pulling a horse's head off to that side. You

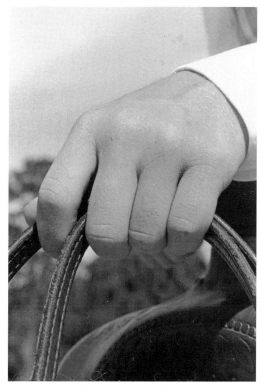

*Place the index finger between split reins, being careful to maintain the correct hand position. If the rider brings the thumb up and turns the knuckles on the vertical, one rein will become shorter than the other.*

*Note that the split reins are crossed over the horse's neck and that both reins are held in each hand. This allows a rider to be more specific with the rein cues, yet remain aware that both hands must work in unison at all times.*

may not notice it much when traveling straightaway, but it will become more obvious when the horse's head gets out of position during a turn.

2/ To use reins with a romal, clinch your hand into a fist around both reins, with the thumb up. The reins run from the bottom of the fist, up and over the thumb. With your other hand, grasp the romal about 16 to 18 inches away from your rein hand and rest this hand on your thigh. When using reins and romal, your rein hand will be carried more over the horn than in front of it, as is the case with split reins.

At some point, you'll probably use two hands on the reins, rather than one. Using both hands on your split reins, with them crossed over a horse's neck, for example, can aid in effectively reinforcing a cue for a specific maneuver. Or, if you plan to rope or barrel race, you'll be using a roping rein, a single continuous rein, rather than split reins. Your hands will be positioned much the same in either case.

When using both hands on a rope rein or split reins, each hand will be in a fist, with the rein coming from underneath, through the palm of the hand, and over the top of the fist. Carry the hands a little to either side of a horse's neck. Think of your arm, from hand to elbow, as an extension of the rein.

Your hands should not be tightly clinched in a death grip on the rein; such tension will be felt by the horse. Nor should you be so relaxed that you're limp-wristed and loose-fingered on the reins; that's not an effective way to communicate with a horse. Just close your fists around the reins securely, not too tightly nor too loosely.

If you're using split reins and riding two-handed, cross the reins over the horse's neck and hold them on the doubled portion. This way, you become more conscious that both hands must work together, giving cues and reinforcing them, even though each hand controls a separate rein.

When using two hands on the reins, take care not to "drive" your horse, using the reins as you would a steering wheel. To do so puts a horse's head in an incorrect position to turn. Should you turn left, steering with the right hand moving counter-clockwise and over the left, it brings a horse's nose to the right—not to the left, the desired direction.

To be more effective, use the two reins in a somewhat parallel manner. Stroke the right rein across a horse's neck to indicate a left turn, and use the left rein, if necessary, to reinforce the cue or to keep a horse's nose properly positioned in the direction of the turn.

# Cues and Reinforcement

When you start riding, the more consistent your cues are, the faster and more consistently a horse learns to give the desired response. As always, you are the herd boss. Insist that the horse respect you, just as you did when handling him from the ground. Again, you use cues or apply pressure to indicate what you want from the horse. Release the pressure when the horse responds as you wish.

When riding, cue your horse by using your voice, your hands on the reins, or your feet and legs. Cue lightly, but firmly, at first, perhaps giving a vocal command. If necessary, reinforce a vocal command with a rein cue or leg cue. When you cue lightly and then reinforce the cue, your horse will eventually operate on the lighter cue. He learns that the cue will become stronger until he performs as desired. If you find it necessary to reinforce a cue, do so emphatically, using firm, intense motions. It is far easier on both you and the horse to correct him sharply for 3 seconds than to nag at him annoyingly for 30 minutes.

Don't lose patience and let frustration take over, even if you must reinforce a cue repeatedly. Remember, especially at first, that you are establishing yourself as boss. Your first horse will test you from time to time. Don't take it personally; most horses test their riders, even the most experienced horsemen, somewhat. Your first horse isn't treating you any differently than he would any horseman.

The difference between you and another horseman, however, lies in how each responds to the challenge. You'll get the best results and maintain more control of the horse by thinking and riding through a problem when a horse tests you. When you lose control of your emotions, you abdicate your position as herd boss and give control to the horse. You are reacting to him, rather than putting him in a position to respond to you.

# Starting and Stopping

The most-used voice commands, for example, are a cluck for forward motion and whoa for a stop. Think of your legs and feet as the accelerator; use them to get a horse moving or to demand additional speed in a maneuver. Use your hands on the reins to steer the motion in the direction you want to go, or as the brakes, to slow or stop the movement.

Should you cluck and a horse respond sluggishly, for example, use your legs and feet to reinforce the cue, accelerating him forward into a more active response. The cluck is the initial light cue; kicking with your feet is the stronger reinforcement. Once a horse is moving at the desired speed, quit reinforcing the cluck cue and give him relief from the pressure of your feet and legs. Only when he fails to maintain the pace should you cue him again. And, again, start with the lighter cue, giving him ample time to respond before reinforcing it.

If you say whoa, for example, and a horse fails to stop promptly, use your reins to reinforce the cue. But be sure to say whoa first and give him the opportunity to respond. If he doesn't stop, apply pressure with your hands to the bit, to reinforce the voice command, whoa. Release the pressure immediately when the horse stops. This is his reward, the relief from pressure, that he earns for responding well.

Novice riders often experience trouble when a horse "prop-stops" on stiffened front legs and with his back hollowed. He should stop softly with his spine rounded and relaxed, which is easier to ride than a prop-stop. Generally a horse who stops hard on the front end has learned to do so because he had no indication that a stop was planned. The rider simply pulls on the reins without saying whoa, or applies pressure to the bit before saying whoa. As a result, the horse is caught unprepared to stop and stiffens his body.

By saying whoa first, before pulling on the reins, you give a horse a few seconds to better position himself for a stop. After all, he does have about 1,000 pounds in motion and four legs to position, rather than two.

Those few seconds better enable him to find the best place in his stride for stopping his motion, no matter what the gait. As a result, he uses his body more effectively, and you experience an easier ride.

Make a habit of saying whoa and then counting to three—before pulling on the reins. Over time, a prop-stopping horse often can learn to be more relaxed in his stop. He is no longer caught unaware, and the few seconds between whoa and the rein cue enable him to make the maneuver easier on himself.

Sometimes a horse becomes lazy in responding to the whoa cue. He slows, but doesn't stop, perhaps not even stopping when you have reinforced the vocal cue with pressure on the reins. In this case, don't continue pulling on the reins; he will only pull harder against your hand. Instead, release the pressure on the reins briefly and reapply the pressure even more forcefully. Do this several times if necessary to ensure that you can safely stop the horse. A horse usually responds better to several increasingly intense cues, or tugs, rather than one long, continuous pull.

# Conflicting Cues

Be sure, in any maneuver, that you are not giving a horse conflicting cues with your hands and feet. When reinforcing a cluck by kicking him forward, for example, don't grip the reins so tightly, applying pressure to the bit, that he thinks you want him to stop. You must release the pressure from the reins to open the door for him to move forward.

On the other hand, when you reinforce whoa by applying pressure to the reins, don't squeeze a horse in the belly with your legs in an effort to hold on. That only leaves him uncertain as to whether he should stop or go. Good horsemanship not only requires consistency in cueing your horse, it also requires that you do so in the least confusing manner possible.

*Maintain proper hand position, as shown, when you cue for the turn. If you roll the hand over as you cue, the horse's head gets out of position as a result.*

# Turning

Your first horse probably turns better in one direction than the other. And, it's probably to the left. That's not unusual. Many horses seem to be left-handed when turning, just as most people are right-handed.

It's simpler to turn a horse in the direction easiest for him to perform the maneuver. However, a horseman's response is to "even up a horse's sides" by turning a horse more often in the difficult direction. Over time, the practice enables the horse to more easily turn to the once-difficult direction. In other words, he's more even in his performance, turning equally well in either direction. A better mount results, one who can carry his rider where he wants to go. The rider isn't forced to adjust his plans because his horse lacks maneuverability.

To turn your horse to the left, bring your rein hand across the horse's neck, from right to left. The right rein applies pressure to his neck and blocks movement to the right; the left rein becomes slack, which opens the door for the horse to move in that direction. Do the reverse to turn to the right, moving the rein across the horse's neck from left to right.

Whether you are riding with split reins or a romal and reins, it's important to use your rein hand correctly.

With split reins, if you roll your thumb up as you signal for the turn, the horse's head gets out of position. In a left turn, for example, rolling your hand results a shorter right rein, which pulls the horse's nose up and to the right—not the desired direction. By keeping your reins even in the turn, the right rein effectively blocks movement in that direction, without restricting the horse's head as he moves in a new direction of travel.

With a romal and reins, your fist is clinched around the reins, with the thumb up. Just as when using split reins, rolling your hand out of the proper position, in either direction, will result in the horse's head being out of position during the turn. Ideally, his nose should be slightly tipped into the turn.

Should your horse not readily turn on command and show resistance in turning, use your outside foot to reinforce the rein cue. For a left turn, kick with your right foot, to drive him in the direction you want to go. Be sure you are not blocking his path of travel or confusing him by using the left foot. The opposite holds true for a right-hand turn.

If necessary, use two hands on the reins to reinforce the turn cue. When going to the left, for example, use one hand on each rein, but work them together at first to signal for the turn. At resistance, reinforce the cue with your right foot, to encourage movement to the left. If that doesn't work, reapply the rein cue. This time, however, as you stroke the reins to the left, apply pressure to the left rein and then release it, using short, quick motions.

In this case, the right rein is the indirect rein, which provides the first, more subtle cue. The left is the direct rein and is used more forcefully to reinforce the original signal. Remember, don't try to outpull the horse; that will only result in a tug-of-war.

Again, be sure you are not giving conflicting cues. Don't take your reins up so short that they block any motion whatever. That confuses a horse even more.

120

Even worse, when carried to an extreme, a horse often begins backing or threatening to rear in this situation. He knows he must move in some direction, but his motion has been effectively blocked in all directions but to the rear.

Be sure, when you ask a horse to turn, that you are giving him enough slack in the reins so that he can move into the turn. When your horse is moving forward and you cue for a turn, you aren't asking him to stop, but to redirect his motion. You must open a door in that direction of travel, not block it with pressure on the reins.

# Walking

To cue for a walk, cluck and shift your weight ever so slightly forward. Your horse should move out on cue. If he doesn't, cluck again, still keeping your weight forward, and bump him in the sides with both feet. Also be sure that you have released any pressure from the reins, which would block his forward motion. Continue to cluck and bump his sides harder until he is walking at the speed you desire. Once the gait has been established, your body position will become more upright as your center of balance settles over the horse's center of balance—at that speed.

# Trotting

When you ask for a trot, again use the same cues, only more intensely. Sitting a two-beat trot is a more jarring proposition that sitting a four-beat walk. Think of yourself as having "jelly in the belly" when riding at a trot. Let the jelly absorb the shock and cushion the motion. There is no way to comfortably sit a trot, especially if the horse has a rough trot, when your spine and lower back are stiff; fluid, supple motion is the key. Don't stiffen your knees and ankles against the jar of a trot. Instead, ride with a relaxed knee and flex your ankles with the motion.

You can also post to the trot for a more comfortable ride. Remember, the trot is a two-beat, diagonal gait. To post to the trot, rise from the saddle as the horse strides forward (beat one) and return to the saddle with the second beat. Don't force

*Horse trainer Craig Johnson uses two hands to make a turn. The initial cue comes from the indirect rein against the horse's neck, but Johnson can reinforce the cue with a direct pull on the left rein if necessary.*

the motion or fight it; let the momentum push you up naturally.

When trotting a lefthand circle, for example, the inside hind (the left) leg and outside foreleg (the right) move simultaneously. By rising in the saddle as these two legs move forward, you will be posting on the correct diagonal. Let your weight follow the action of these legs, shifting back into the saddle as the stride is completed. When circling to the right, do the opposite; rise when the right hind and left front legs advance. It helps to watch the horse's outside shoulder, rising as it moves forward, when learning to post.

Because the two-beat gait is jarring, you become more aware of rating a horse's speed in the trot. If your first horse is like many, he will probably continue to trot faster until you indicate that he should hold the gait at a certain speed. First, be sure that you are relaxed in the saddle. You may be leaning forward, which indicates an increase in speed to most horses.

If that's not the case, pick up the reins

*Upper body control is important in maintaining correct body position, no matter what a horse is doing. In this series, Scott McCutcheon uses his arm to emphasize the position of his upper body. A rider leans forward to cue a horse to move out or for more speed.*

*McCutcheon's body, more straightly aligned here, signals the horse to continue working as is. Leaning forward or back, however, would help signal the horse to increase or decrease his speed.*

The rider leans back somewhat to indicate to the
horse that a back-up is the
next maneuver, as shown,
or to signal that a stop is
planned.

and apply pressure to the bit to rate your
horse to a slower trot. Don't tighten the
pressure on the reins and hold them continually. Rating a horse requires give-and-
take. You take the slack out of the reins,
and he gives by reducing his speed. You
then release the pressure on the reins to
give relief. At first, it may be necessary to
reinforce a rate cue repeatedly until your
horse understands to hold the trot at a
given speed. Do not, however, say whoa
when you rate his speed back. This only
confuses a horse who has been taught to
stop at the whoa command.

## Loping

By now, you've figured out that good
horsemanship is mastered one step at the
time, with each step laying the foundation
to safely progress to the next one. Yes,
riding can be risky business, but the better
you have prepared yourself to perform a
new maneuver, the more you control the
risks and the horse. Many novice riders
are somewhat hesitant to lope their horses
at first. Once you've found the middle of
your saddle at a walk and a trot, and can
safely stop and turn your horse, loping
him is a real and achievable goal. Don't be

afraid to try it; trust in the foundation
you've laid.

The lope is a three-beat gait, usually
more comfortable to ride than the trot. You
probably remember the earlier discussion
in the chapter on test-riding a prospective
first horse, where leads were discussed.
Understanding leads is important to
improving your horsemanship, but many
people enjoy riding without giving a
thought to loping on the correct lead.
More information on leads will follow, but
first learn to lope your horse in a con-
trolled manner.

If you are a novice rider, concentrate on
establishing the gait when you first lope a
horse. Establishing the gait means that
you can successfully cue a horse to change
gait and hold the new gait for a period of
time, not just for a few strides or halfway
around the arena. Again, consistency is
important—not only in cueing a horse, but
also in requiring him to travel steadily in a
given gait and for a period of time.

Cue a horse to lope much as you do for
a walk or trot, leaning forward and cluck-
ing first. Many horsemen will cluck once

for a walk, but cluck repeatedly and quickly for a trot or lope. Some kick harder and faster when reinforcing the cues to trot or lope. In any case, the important thing is to cue consistently and to use reinforcement consistently. Again, be sure you are not binding the horse's forward motion by applying pressure to the bit, as you cue him to lope.

Once the horse is loping, keep your body well-aligned. Remember: leaning forward usually encourages a horse to go faster; leaning back in the saddle usually slows his motion. Your body should be in a neutral position—as long as he is loping at a consistent speed. Should he speed up, rate him back in the lope, just as you did in the trot. Should he break into a trot, shift your weight forward, using your feet and legs to drive him into a lope.

Novice riders often are concerned about a horse running away when he's loping. It isn't wise to try loping until you are sure that you can stop a horse—that he understands whoa. But even the best broke horses can become frightened and choose flight, rather than fight, when something scares them. Nor does a horse have to be in a dead run for a novice rider to feel that he's participating in a runaway. A "trot-away" can be as frightening an experience to a child as a real runaway is to an experienced horseman.

If all else fails, there's an emergency brake that usually works with most horses when you feel you have lost control. To safely handle a potential runaway, don't panic or throw the reins away. Simply steer the horse in a circle.

For most people, it's easier to turn in the same direction as the rein hand. If you ride left-handed, steer left, or vice-versa. Don't worry about how much pressure you're using on the bit. This is not the time to be kind; it's time to safely control a potentially bad situation. If necessary, put both hands on the left rein, for example, and pull the horse's head around to your knee. It takes some effort to steer him into progressively smaller circles, but you can probably bring the horse under control.

**For a horse to willingly move on command into a blind spot, he must have total faith in his herd boss.**

Simply put, you bind the horse's forward motion into a turn, making it more difficult for him to take a well-balanced, straightforward running stride. If you feel the need, trot your horse and test the procedure. Don't say whoa, simply pull his head around with one hand, drawing him into smaller and smaller circles. Forward motion will cease, and if the circles are tight enough, the horse will stop altogether.

## Leads

When you can comfortably maintain a lope and stop on command, you're ready to learn about leads and how to cue for a specific one.

To better understand leads, stand behind another person and grip his waist with your hands. The two of you should try to skip in unison, either to the left or right. If you move well in unison, you're both on the same lead. If the movement is rough and uncoordinated, you are "cross-loping," with one of you leading with the left foot and the other with the right.

If, when you test-rode your horse, you learned that he can take either lead, there is an additional cue you will need to practice until it becomes habitual. Most horses trained to take a specific lead are cued to do so with the rider's outside foot. For example, if you are loping a counter-clockwise circle to the left, your horse should be on the left lead. You cue for the left lead by applying pressure with your right, or outside, foot. For a right lead, cue with the left foot. If the horse doesn't lope immediately, kick harder with the outside foot.

By using the outside foot to cue for a lead, you are, in effect, positioning a horse's body to move more effectively in a given direction. The pressure from your foot pushes a horse's rear end into the circle, making it easier for him to pick up the correct lead. Novices are often told to pull a horse's head to the outside of the circle, as they cue for a specific lead. The effect is the same whether you push his rear end in or pull his front end out; you better position the horse to give the right response.

It's difficult at first for a novice to tell which lead a horse is loping on. But by watching the movement of his shoulders, you can eventually see the difference. It's often easier to look at your own feet. When loping on the left lead, your left foot tends to be positioned somewhat ahead of your right foot. On the right lead, your right foot will hang more forward. To best learn about leads, have an experienced horseman watch while you lope a horse. A knowledgeable person can tell you when you are in a specific lead, and you can better learn the difference between the two leads.

Just as when making a turn, most horses tend to prefer the left lead. And, just as with turning, you can even up a horse's sides. To do so, it's necessary to work the horse more on the poorer-leaded side. If he's harder to get into the right lead, ask him to lope on the right lead more often than you do the left. Eventually he will become coordinated and skilled in traveling on the right lead.

# Backing

Not all horses back readily on command. This is not an equine whim. Remember learning about a horse's range of vision? He can't see directly behind himself; that's his blind spot. For a horse to willingly move on command into a blind spot, he must have total faith in his herd boss. In effect, a horse takes your word for it that there is nothing in the blind spot that will hurt him.

To back a horse, pick up the reins, using light, but equal pressure on both, and lean back slightly. Some horses, well-trained to back, often require no more cue than that before backing. Reining horses often back on such a light cue and increase their speed as the rider clucks. More often, however, a horse is somewhat sluggish in responding to the cue for backing. If that's the case, reinforce the cue much as you would reinforce a rate cue or a turn signal, applying and releasing pressure on the reins in increasingly quick movements.

When you pick up the reins to cue for a back-up, you take the slack from the reins, which, in effect, blocks a horse's forward motion. And, possibly, your horse can stand still for quite a while, with slight pressure on the reins. But, by repeatedly applying pressure more forcefully and then releasing it, you make it uncomfortable for a horse to remain at a standstill. In

other words, the right thing, the back-up, becomes easier than the wrong thing—not moving at all.

Remember, it takes time for a horse to learn to be more responsive in any maneuver, so don't lose patience during the first few attempts or even the first days or weeks of work. A horse learns slowly through repetition, so the more consistent and methodical you are in using cues and reinforcement, the more quickly a horse learns to give the desired response.

*Texas trainer Scott McCutcheon demonstrates the difference when a horse is on the right lead (top) and a left lead (bottom).*

# COMMON PROBLEMS

## 14

*Horses can have a sour attitude about leaving a buddy in open country, just as they can become barn-soured when leaving the horse in an adjoining stall.*

SOMETIMES the more you work at the sport of riding, the more problems you run into. That's because you're trying new things more often, which is good in one respect. The more you ride and the more problems you solve, the better horseman you become. On the other hand, solving the problems can be frustrating.

A few basic guidelines can often see you through many problems. Practice applying them, and you're well on your way to becoming a horseman.

1/ Learn to read your horse so that you can determine whether the problem is the result of his resistance to your authority or to fear. Then you'll better understand how to approach the problem in either case.

2/ Try to make giving the right response easy for the horse and the wrong response more difficult for him.

3/ The solution to a problem often is found in going back to basics, the lessons a horse should have learned during training, but maybe never fully understood.

## Barn-, Trailer-, or Buddy-Soured Horses

Take, for example, a barn-soured horse, who doesn't want to leave the stable area. Why should he leave? His herd mates are there, he gets fed there, and little effort is required of him there.

Few horses fear leaving a barn; most are simply resisting authority. In the previous chapter, it was mentioned that horses often test a new rider, no matter how accomplished a horseman he is. You must decide if that's the case in your situation.

126

If your first horse is broke and trained, it's likely that he's simply testing you somewhat, to find out how willing you are to take control as herd boss and make him leave the barn.

If you're reasonably certain the horse understands what you want, and is resisting your authority, then you probably haven't been tough enough in reinforcing your cues for him to get the message that you are in control. Don't think of taking control as being abusive. If you continue riding, sooner or later, your safety or that of your horse may well depend on your ability to take control and to have your horse respond well to your direction.

Take control of a barn-soured horse by making the right thing—leaving the barn—easier than the wrong thing—staying there. You should be forceful, determined, and consistent in reinforcing your cues until you get the response you want. Kick him harder when you ask him to move out or swat him on the rump with the bridle reins. Do whatever it takes to make staying at the barn the most uncomfortable option for the horse.

Another possible solution is putting the horse to work right there in front of the barn. Demand some effort from him. Long trot or lope circles. Periodically, let him walk, but in a direction away from the barn. If he's not willing, make him work harder. When you let him walk, aim him away from the barn. Soon he will find it less taxing to leave than to stay.

The important thing is that the horse finds relief as soon as he moves away from the barn. You must give him relief from whatever pressure you have applied in getting the response you want. He will learn that it is more pleasant, in this case, away from the barn than it is nearby. He also learns that relief from pressure is the reward for making a correct response to your commands.

Conversely, some horses leave the barn willingly enough but, the minute you head back after a riding session, rush toward it, going faster and faster. Rating the horse's speed seems to have little meaning to him at this point. He wants back in the barn where his buddies are, where he's fed and comfortable.

Don't let him take you to the barn and then dismount there. That only reinforces, in his mind, the idea that rushing home is the right thing to do. He finds a reward there; you dismount and put him up.

Instead, teach your horse that he finds his reward away from the barn. After a training session, for example, on a riding track or in an arena away from the barn, step off your horse there, and then walk him to the barn. Or when you return from a trail ride, pick a spot some distance from

**Remember, too, that the first time you work at correcting such a problem is usually the most difficult.**

the barn for dismounting. It shouldn't be the same place every time, or your horse will learn to rush there, just as he would to the barn, expecting you to dismount.

In an extreme situation, if a horse takes you home in a hurry, don't dismount. Again, put the horse to work right there in front of the barn. Periodically, ride a distance from the barn and then try walking the horse toward it. You'll know when you have made your point; he won't rush to the barn any longer. Instead of finding the expected relief from work there, he's had to work harder, so hurrying home is no longer the easiest option for him.

Some novice riders unknowingly encourage the bad habit of galloping back to the barn. How? Riders who like to "go fast" find it difficult to make their horses lope or gallop away from the barn, or out on a trail ride. But these riders quickly learn that horses will willingly gallop toward the barn. So when these riders want to go fast, they point their horses toward the barn. After only a few runs back to the barn, these horses become like race horses in a starting gate. Point them toward the barn, and they're off. They have developed a dangerous habit through no fault of their own. Always walk back to the barn.

If you haul your new horse regularly to ride with friends or to a playday, remember that the trailer becomes your horse's barn away from home. The trailer is the place he now finds pleasant, where he is unsaddled and fed or watered. So don't consistently dismount at your trailer when you're away from home. Dismount elsewhere, then lead your horse to the trailer and tie him.

Too, horses can become soured to leav-

ing their herd mates when out on the trail, just as they can become barn-soured or trailer-soured. A similar approach often works with the horse who doesn't want to leave his buddy. Again, make the right thing—leaving the herd mate—easier than the wrong thing—staying near his buddy—by reinforcing your commands more strongly as you ride away from the other horse.

Or, perhaps, make the horse work harder physically while circling the other horse in larger and larger circles. Periodically direct your horse away from his buddy. If your mount is unhappy about it, continue working him. Don't give him relief until he is away from his friend. Then let him relax. Again, this doesn't mean you abuse the horse by running him out of air; he is simply not allowed to relax and find total rest or relief until he is some distance from the other horse.

There are no overnight solutions to correcting a barn-, trailer-, or buddy-soured horse. However, by being consistent and firm in dealing with the problem, you probably can make progress in solving it and in establishing yourself as the boss.

Remember, too, that the first time you work at correcting such a problem is usually the most difficult, the point where you will meet the most resistance from the horse. Meeting such a challenge to your authority becomes easier with time. You have everything to gain by assuming command in such situations—and everything to lose if you don't.

## Turning Problems

Another problem novice riders encounter has been discussed in the previous chapter, such as meeting resistance when you ask the horse to turn left, for example. You learned to use a neck-rein cue.

You also found that you can reinforce the neck rein cue by driving the horse into the turn with the outside (right) leg, for example, or by using the left, or direct rein, to make the response you want even more clear to the horse. You also know to reverse these procedures for making a right-hand turn.

These reinforcement tactics often work on a broke, trained horse, who is, perhaps, a little slow in responding to an initial cue. However, if you meet extreme resistance in making a turn, there are other considerations.

Again, you must decide if your horse is testing you. If you're sure a horse understands the cue, but he's not turning, then possibly you haven't reinforced the cue strongly enough. Often a show of strength on your part results in a horse caving in to your authority, accepting that you're the boss. Again, make the right thing—turning—easier than the wrong thing—resisting your cue. Be forceful, determined, and consistent in reinforcing your cue.

Don't worry too much about being challenged, when making a turn, by your new horse. If he truly is the right kind of first horse, he'll probably respond as most trained horses do: "Oh well, I can't get away with it. . . . I'll just go on and turn."

Another consideration: Whenever you experience a breakdown in communicating with your horse, it's important to check your equipment. Is the headstall properly adjusted for the bit to hang correctly in the horse's mouth? Is the curb strap set correctly? Feel your bit. Is there a rough spot in the metal that could be causing discomfort? If you are using a loose-shanked bit, check the butt of the mouthpiece to ensure that the joints are smooth and not so worn that the horse is being pinched during a maneuver.

No matter what age your horse, have your veterinarian check his mouth for wolf teeth or other dental problems. The bit could be bumping a wolf tooth, for example, which can result in head-sling-

*When a horse responds poorly to a turn cue, and you're riding with one hand on the reins, it often helps to reinforce the turn cue by using two hands on the reins. The rider first cues for the turn with the left rein, then reinforces the cue, using the direct right rein.*

*It isn't always necessary to cross the reins over the neck when using two hands on the reins to reinforce a turn cue. Although she had been using only the left hand on both reins, the rider can immediately reinforce the cue by using the right hand on the rein as shown.*

ing as the horse tries to evade pressure in a sensitive area.

Another serious problem in turning results when a horse has failed to understand a basic lesson—how to yield to pressure. He should understand that giving to the pressure applied to a bit brings relief. This is fundamental in developing a responsive mount.

If your horse resists a neck-rein cue and seems unsure of the response you want, it's possible that he squeaked through his learn-to-give-to-the-pressure lessons when he was broke and trained. He may have given to the pressure occasionally or by accident, without really understanding the desired response. If you suspect that's the case, here's a simple exercise that can help improve any horse's response, no matter what the maneuver or how trained the horse.

You and the horse are going back to primary school, so you will handle him much like a trainer starting a colt does. With the horse standing still, use two hands on the reins of a snaffle bit.

If the problem is in turning left, for example, pick up the left rein, and hold steady pressure on the rein. That's right—hold. You'll probably feel resistance as the horse balks at turning his head. That's a dead giveaway that he doesn't give well to pressure. Continue holding the rein, tipping the horse's nose into the turn. You needn't be too forceful; just ask the horse to give his head a little to the left. It may take several minutes, the first few times you try this exercise, for the horse to yield to the pressure.

Be sure that you are not blocking any motion by holding the indirect rein (right) so tightly that the horse is not free to move and turn his head to the left.

Sooner or later, most horses will give to the pressure, relax, and move the head toward your hand. The minute that happens, release your hold and praise the horse, rub his neck, or whatever. This is his reward for responding to the pressure. The more often you do this exercise, the more quickly he comes to understand that to find relief, he must make the right response and give to the pressure.

As he becomes more responsive in giving to the pressure of the direct rein, you can perform the same maneuver at a walk or a trot, asking the horse to give his head to either direction while he maintains forward motion. This further reinforces that idea that he must give to the pressure—even when he's moving—and will help improve his response to handling at any speed.

When your horse's response rate has noticeably increased and he quickly gives to the pressure of the direct rein more often than not, then it's time to try the left turn cue with the indirect rein once again. The difference? Now the reinforcement—using the direct rein—has more meaning to the horse and value to you as a horseman. The horse better understands what you want, and you are better able to correct him.

This exercise can also be helpful in other maneuvers where a horse must respond to pressure on the bit, such as a stop, backup, or circling in a lope. Going back to the basics with a horse often has multiple benefits, and simple exercises such as this one are the tools of the horseman's trade.

# Reinforcing Whoa

More often than not, one of the first problems a new horse owner encounters is a walkaway. That's right, a walkaway. The horse walks off when he should be standing still, often when the rider is mounting or dismounting.

Again, a horse is a creature of habit. If he is allowed to ignore the whoa command and walk away when being mounted, for example, sooner or later he will ignore the whoa command at a trot or a lope. Why shouldn't he? He tried walking off and it worked. If your whoa command isn't working at a standstill or from a walk or a trot, it will eventually fail you when you're loping. For safety's sake, demand that your horse respect whoa at all times.

For instance, when you mount your horse and he takes several steps before you're settled in the saddle, don't ignore the problem. Right then is the time to correct the problem, before it gets more pronounced.

Should your horse step out as you mount, step down and prepare to mount him again. This time be sure you have the reins short enough to make quick contact with the bit when he walks off. As you mount and he moves, quietly say whoa. If he ignores whoa, immediately reinforce the command, using the reins to stop his forward motion. This may well happen before you are completely in the saddle. If so, simply raise your left hand from the withers to apply pressure to the bit, making sure you have a good grip on the horn with your right.

Once the horse stops, prepare to mount again, and repeat the whoa command, reinforcing it with rein pressure when necessary.

Usually, after several such corrections, most horses will stand for you to mount. Standing still, the right thing, is easier than walking away, the wrong thing. If necessary, mount and dismount six or seven times, never letting him move. He will soon wise up and stand still.

To prevent this problem from happening, never let a horse move until you are settled in the saddle, and then you ask him to begin moving. If he's continually allowed to move off when he wants to, you have created the problem.

Stopping a horse isn't so much a problem sometimes as is getting him to stand quietly afterwards. Teaching a horse to stand quietly is not a process that can be rushed. It requires persistence and consistency on your part, as does any schooling you do with your horse.

If you have a habit of rushing maneuvers, your horse will develop a similar one as well.

*Stopping in mid-mount is sometimes necessary when reinforcing the whoa command to ensure that a horse stands still for mounting and dismounting.*

Sometimes a horse stops on command, stands a moment or two, and then walks off whether the rider has cued him or not. This often results when a rider habitually hurries his mount, rushing from one maneuver to the next. Be sure that you haven't developed a habit of stopping your horse and immediately requesting another maneuver, without pausing after the stop. If you have a habit of rushing maneuvers, your horse will develop a similar one as well.

All too often, a rider says whoa and pulls on the reins a little when a horse walks out of a stop. The horse ignores the little pull and keeps walking. The rider pulls a little more steadily, and the horse pulls back against the bit, but never quits walking. The problem escalates and, before long, the rider is hanging on the horse's mouth, applying steady pressure to try to hold the horse as he walks out of a stop.

The rider in this situation has failed to properly reinforce the whoa command, and a pulling contest has resulted. Remember, few people are stout enough to out-pull a horse. You can, however, use quick, sharp tugs on the reins to reinforce the whoa command, becoming progressively more forceful, if necessary, to get the horse's attention. A horse usually will give to such pressure, rather than pulling against it.

When the horse stops, pressure on the bit should be released completely. Most horses accustomed to walking out of a stop will immediately take a step forward when the pressure is released. Don't become angry; it took some time for this habit to develop, and it will likely take you some time to change it.

Simply say whoa again, reinforce the command more strongly, and give relief from the pressure when the horse makes the right response. For a more resistant horse, it may be necessary to back him a few steps to further reinforce the whoa command.

It probably will take several such corrections over several days' time for your horse to learn to stand with slack in the reins. If at all possible during the correction process, try to relax each time the horse stands, for however short a time, rather than tensely expecting him to step out. If the rider takes a deep breath when giving slack in the reins, it often encourages a horse to relax and stand. Just as a horseman learns to read his horse and recognize fear or resistance, most horses read their riders. If you are unable to relax and sit still, your horse will read and feed off your emotions and find it difficult to stand still.

The whoa command is important to your safety. Don't neglect to use it properly with your horse. If, for example, you have trouble stopping your horse when loping, consider what you have learned so far.

First, be sure you are cueing the horse correctly for a stop. Then reinforce the cues more strongly, being sure to give relief from the pressure when a horse gives the correct response. Ask your horse to stop politely the first time or two, and then tell him to stop when he fails to respond. You are the boss, and you must take control.

You can also go back to basics in this situation. If you're having difficulty getting an immediate response to whoa when loping, slow down. Trot the horse, say whoa, and see what kind of response you get.

If he stops immediately from a trot, you probably aren't reinforcing the whoa command firmly enough when loping. Try loping again, but be tougher and more demanding when you stop your horse.

If, however, the horse doesn't stop well when trotting, slow down again, and see if he responds to whoa when walking. A walkaway can well be the foundation on which a poor stop from a lope is built. So walk and stop your horse several times, or for several days. Do whatever is necessary to ensure that he understands the whoa command at a walk.

Once you're satisfied that a horse understands whoa when walking, increase his speed to a trot. Follow much the same procedure when trotting. Again, take whatever time is necessary to develop an immediate stop from a trot, and reinforce the cue as firmly as necessary to get the job done.

When a horse responds well when trotting, and stops quickly the majority of the time, check his response at a lope. If the response isn't as immediate as you would like, trot and stop some more before loping again. You are, in effect, brainwashing your horse to stop on the whoa command. The more thorough you are when laying the foundation at a walk and a trot, the more likely you are to get the desired response at a lope.

# Another Option

There are, however, some horses so "soured" in a particular maneuver, such as turning in one direction, that you may need a professional to help you solve a deep-rooted problem.

If you strongly and repeatedly reinforce a cue without results, give some thought to the response you see. Does the horse pin his ears back flatly in obvious resentment to your command and stiffen his body in resistance? Have you been as tough as you have the nerve to be, without seeing improvement? Have you reinforced the basics without results?

You may well be able to find a solution to the problem yourself—over a period of time, but it's also possible that you may compound a problem through your lack of experience. A professional can help you avoid many common mistakes and make the most effective use of your riding time. He can target the problem and help you focus more immediately on a solution. The cost of professional assistance will seem small when compared to the frustrations sometimes experienced when mastering a new skill on your own. The next chapter takes a look at lessons and trainers.

# LESSONS AND TRAINERS

# 15

FEW THINGS can benefit a novice horseman more than spending some time with a knowledgeable riding instructor or horse trainer.

A horse, though most often a forgiving creature, is not a machine or instrument with no memory of the mistakes made during the learning process. A mistake at the piano, for example, can be corrected by playing the right note; the piano isn't a living thing that reacts to how forcefully or timidly the note is struck. But, when a mistake is made in horsemanship, the correction process, unless handled properly, can add to a horse's resistance to or fear of performing.

Of course, many people like to be able to say, "I did it myself," when learning something new. It's an admirable approach, but seldom the most direct one to mastering good horsemanship. Horses come complete with inherent characteristics and individual personalities, so to speak, so the approach that works well with one horse won't necessarily work with another. There is no perfect textbook horse, just as there are no cut-and-dried instructions for riding one successfully. This often makes it difficult for a novice horseman to solve the problems he encounters when learning to ride. The novice doesn't have a data base of horsemanship experience to research for solutions, as does a professional.

Professional horsemen work with many horses, trying many methods and techniques to get a desired response. More important, few professionals ever dis-

*The cones and tires around the barrel are only a few of the many aids instructors such as R.E. Josey of Karnack Tex., use to help students improve their riding.*

count a technique simply because it didn't work with an individual horse at a given time; a top hand saves the method for future reference. It is this knowledge that makes the professional an invaluable asset to the novice rider, who can seldom devote his full-time efforts toward gathering such knowledge.

Finding the right riding instructor is much like finding the right first horse to buy; the process may be a quick one, or it may take some time. You probably learned of some instructors during your first horse search. If so, you have a place to start. If not, cover the same ground again and call stables, tack shops, veterinarian offices, or feed stores to get names of area instructors. Attend a local playday or horse show and ask the accomplished riders, both adults and children, if they are working with an instructor.

Call potential instructors and, again, be honest and explain that you are a first-time horse owner. Some instructors take only beginners; others take only accomplished riders working in specific events, such as barrel racing or trail classes. Ask whether individual instruction or group lessons are offered, what lessons cost, the average time required for a lesson, and whether your horse or a school horse is used for the lessons. Due to liability considerations, some instructors no longer maintain school horses; others, however, do.

If at all possible, use your own horse during the lessons. Then, when you do encounter a problem or challenge from your new mount, and you will, the instructor can help you ride through the problem and find a solution all the more quickly. Such firsthand experience is invaluable in putting you and your new horse together as a team.

On the other hand, school horses are often so steady and dependable that a novice rider is better able to devote attention to the instruction itself, rather than worrying about what the horse might do. If you are a true novice with no grasp of how to handle or cue a horse and have yet to find the middle of the saddle, a school horse might be more forgiving of your mistakes. Such horses, after all, have a high tolerance for rider error. Once you have become comfortable handling the school horse, you will be better prepared to apply your newfound knowledge to your own horse.

*Riding instruction can help anyone at any level of experience become a better horseman. Here, Candy Rodewald of Colorado Springs assists a student at a 4-H horsemanship clinic.*

Ask, too, if you can audit a lesson at the instructor's place of business. It will give you a better opportunity to assess the student-teacher relationship, as the instructor interprets it. Nor is it unreasonable to ask an instructor for references. Talking with current and former students gives you a better idea of how well your personality and the instructor's will mesh.

Whether you are seeking instruction for yourself or for a child, don't overlook the personality factor. Different teaching methods work better with different individuals, and compatibility between student and teacher yields more satisfaction and riding success.

If incompatibility becomes a problem, likely the instructor has noticed it, too. There's nothing wrong with leaving one instructor to work with another. Remember, though, that mastering horsemanship is not an overnight thing, and be sure that the student, horse, and instructor have had ample time to demonstrate progress before making a change.

*When receiving instruction, the emphasis is sometimes on the horse's performance and, at other times, focuses on the rider.*

Generally, there is a set price per lesson for a specific period of time, and a discount may be offered for those signing up for a series of lessons. Should your instructor haul your horse to an event, or help you with special grooming, such as clipping or shortening a mane, there could be additional charges on your bill. Maintaining a good student-teacher relationship is far easier when both clearly understand what services are being offered and at what price.

This also holds true when a trainer works with your horse. Understand what services are included within the training fee. Many trainers charge a flat fee to work with a horse on a 30-day basis, providing a regularly cleaned stall for your horse, along with grain and hay.

Should farrier work or veterinary services be required when your horse is at training barn, you will be responsible for those bills. Should the trainer haul and show your horse at your request, the entry fees, transportation costs, and such are additional expenses and you will be billed for your share. Cutting horse trainers, who

must have cattle on hand to work the horses, often add a cattle charge to the bill.

Many trainers consider instructing you as part of the service when they hire on to ride for you. Other trainers, however, charge extra for anything more than the briefest instruction. One trainer might welcome drop-in visits from his customers and be flexible enough to work with you and your horse almost any time. With another trainer, dropping by the barn may well interfere with his work and other paying customers. Again, ask questions until you fully understand what to expect when taking your horse to a trainer.

Why take a horse to a trainer? Most often, a rider has repeatedly confronted what, to him, is an unsolvable problem in getting his horse to perform as desired. It may be as simple as a horse who won't stand still when being mounted, or as dangerous as a horse the rider cannot control. Or, the rider may realize his mount doesn't truly understand a maneuver, such as taking the right lead or backing up, and the rider feels too inexperienced to deal with the problem.

Some horse owners are too busy to ride regularly, but still desire a fit, responsive mount for weekend shows. A horse could simply be unsuitable for the rider or for the type riding he prefers. In this case, the sooner a horse owner learns and accepts that, the more quickly he can find an appropriate mount.

Worst of all are the few outlaw horses, who have more problems than the first-time horse owner can deal with. A professional should be honest if this is the case, and most are. After all, he doesn't want you hurt at his barn any more than you do.

As with purchasing a horse, hiring a trainer or a riding instructor should come with a label warning the buyer to beware. Most industry professionals are just that—professional in the way their business is handled. Some, though, are not and take advantage of the first-time horse owner's lack of knowledge, charging him for services not rendered or stretching lessons or training out far longer than necessary. As best you can,

*Candy Rodewald, who often conducts clinics herself, works to improve her barrel racing techniques with clinician Sharon Camarillo of Lockeford, California.*

know who you are dealing with and rely on guidance from someone you trust.

Do not, however, be dismayed if a well-recommended trainer tells you that it could take 60 days or longer to accomplish what you want done with your horse. Good training is not accomplished overnight, and the trainer was likely being honest with you. After all, he won't look good if you don't look good when you get your horse back home. Few trainers will work with a horse for less than 30 days, and most prefer at least 60 or more, depending on the level of training required.

If matching a green rider with a green horse is the most common mistake first-time horse owners make, failing to get professional assistance when they need it is probably the second most common error. Paying for lessons or training seems costly at first glance, and the novice often thinks he can eventually resolve a major problem with his horse, and, occasionally, he can. More often than not, however, by

the time the novice decides professional help is required, the problem has been compounded. The rider, with his lack of experience, has only reinforced the horse's bad behavior.

A more direct route to successfully riding a first horse is to seek help early on and take advantage of the experience a pro can bring to your situation.

If you have a problem with your new horse, step back and evaluate the situation. Does a problem truly exist, or is it just a quirk of that horse's behavior that you don't like? Is the problem becoming repetitive, reoccurring on a regular basis? Does the severity of the problem seem to be escalating each time you ride? Is the problem an endangerment to you or your horse? If so, seek help. The money you must pay for lessons or training will be money well spent.

# ADVANCED MANEUVERS

**16**

ALTHOUGH this book has been written for the first-time horse owner and/or the novice horseman, there is more to the art of horsemanship than riding a horse at a walk, trot, or canter. This chapter includes a sampling of the more advanced maneuvers that a well-trained horse and accomplished rider can perform. Even if you don't attempt these maneuvers with your horse, knowledge of them can help you better appreciate the next horse show or horsemanship clinic you attend.

## Simple and Flying Lead Changes

Cueing a horse for loping in the correct lead has been discussed previously, and when a horse changes direction and lopes, he should change leads to move most efficiently.

A simple lead change results when a horse loping to the left, for example, is rated back to a trot when a change of

*This young horsewoman pivoted her mount while performing the maneuvers required during a 4-H test of her horsemanship skills.*

direction is required, and then cued to lope in the right lead as he moves into that new direction of travel. This maneuver is often used in horsemanship or equitation classes where the competitors perform a pattern to display their ability.

A flying lead change requires more skill from both horse and rider than does the simple lead change. The rider doesn't rate the horse to a trot when performing a flying change. Instead, the horse continues to lope, changing leads in mid-flight.

Sometimes used in horsemanship patterns, a flying change is always performed in reining competition where longer and more complex patterns are presented for a judge's evaluation. Speed event horses also perform flying lead changes, because doing so makes for a faster time. Watch a barrel racer approach the first barrel on the right lead, then head for the second barrel where the horse must make a left-hand turn as he runs. At some point between the two barrels, most horses will perform a flying lead change.

# Pivots, Rollbacks, and Spins

It's likely you'll run across the term "pivot" used in connection with an equine sporting event. When performing a pivot, a horse settles his weight over his hindquarters, using them as a pivot point around which his front end travels.

Imagine a horse standing in the center of a circle or on the face of a clock. In performing a quarter-pivot to the right, for example, his haunches would remain at center as his forehand moves 90 degrees around the arc of the circle. At the completion of the maneuver, the horse faces right, toward 3 o'clock, rather than straight ahead in the 12 o'clock position. Cutting horses pivot on their hindquarters as they move to block the cattle.

A rollback combines elements of both the stop and the turn, and a knowledge of leads is important as well. This maneuver is often performed in a reining class. From a gallop, the horse stops, turns 180 degrees about-face, and gallops out. When a horse rolls back to the right, for example, he should lope out of the maneuver on the right lead, and vice versa.

A spin, or turnaround, as it is also called, is a complete 360-degree revolu-

*When performing a spin, or turnaround, the impulsion comes from the hindquarters, which serve as an axis around which the horse rotates. In this sequence of four photos, Craig Johnson of Gainesville, Tex., demonstrates this maneuver using only a bridle rein around the horse's neck.*

*2/ The horse's body position remains relatively straight even though his nose is tipped somewhat in the direction of the spin.*

3/ *The horse steps over with his right front.*

4/ *Performing a turn-around with no bridle demonstrates that this maneuver should be achieved with finesse, not force.*

tion, and the horse again uses his hindquarters as a pivot point.

When a horse spins to the left, his inside hind foot, or left rear foot, is known as the pivot foot and remains relatively stationary during the maneuver. It must, of necessity, be repositioned periodically during the spin, but it remains the pivot point throughout the maneuver. In this example of the spin, the outside front leg, the right, crosses over the left, or inside front leg, in a smooth, rhythmic manner as the forehand travels around the hindquarters. A well-trained horse becomes a blur, performing multiple spins at a high rate of speed.

## The Side-Pass

The side-pass, perhaps, is one of the most useful advanced horsemanship maneuvers. The horse steps sideways, using the forequarters and hindquarters in unison, to maneuver around or through all kinds of obstacles. As in the turnaround, the legs cross over one another. The side-pass is used by showmen, trail riders, and cowboys alike as they approach gates, for example, while mounted, or to navigate around obstacles in their path.

140

1/ This series of photographs demonstrates how to open and close a gate from horseback. The more responsive a horse is in performing the side-pass, the easier it is for the rider to put him into position to handle the gate.

## The Cues

Perhaps you will attend a riding clinic or see a video where flying lead changes, rollbacks, spins, and side-passes are discussed. If so, pay particular attention to how the horseman uses his hands and feet to cue the horse for each maneuver. He applies or releases pressure on the bit with his hands, or to the horse's body with his legs. Although the cues are used in different ways or combinations for each maneuver, the effect is generally the same. Applied pressure blocks the horse's motion or direction of travel, and the release of pressure opens the door to a new direction of travel.

Many riders enjoy their horses without ever having mastered these or other advanced horsemanship maneuvers. But if you're interested in learning more, there are books and videos on the market that describe such maneuvers in step-by-step detail. *WH* books, such as *Reining*, explain in detail how these maneuvers are taught. Attend one of the many horsemanship clinics available through local 4-H or riding clubs and at major equine events. You'll be glad you did.

2/ After pulling the gate toward you to open it, walk around the end while holding the gate with one hand. The horse yields his hindquarters to the right, moving away from the cue (pressure) applied by the left leg.

3/ *After passing through the gate, move far enough forward so the horse's hind-quarters clear the post.*

4/ *Side-passing the horse, pull the gate toward you to close it.*

5/ Then back up to secure the latch or chain on the gate.

# Take a Test

Working a gate is a somewhat complex maneuver to perform, but it's an excellent test of how well your horse responds to commands. Several simple maneuvers are used in combination to open and close a gate when you're mounted. How well you work the gate depends directly on how well you and your horse have mastered basic maneuvers.

To test yourself and your horse's response, approach a gate. Be sure and use at least a 4-foot gate that's properly hung and well-balanced so it is easy for you to control. Working quietly and deliberately, one step at the time, open and close the gate, maintaining your hold on it at all times to prevent it from bumping the horse.

Can you side-pass your horse into position, parallel and close to the gate with his hindquarters toward the hinges? Is he responsive to the whoa command, standing quietly while you lean over and unfasten the gate? Can you move his hindquarters around the forehand as you move from one side of the gate to the other? Can you easily step him forward or back him into position to refasten the gate, as necessary?

After you've worked the gate, you won't need an expert to tell you what to do; the results of this test will be obvious. Your horse's response will tell you if he needs more schooling, for example, on yielding to leg pressure. Or perhaps he understands it in the side-pass, but hasn't quite mastered the concept when moving his hindquarters independently as he turns on the forehand.

Whatever the problem, don't grill your horse, working the gate repeatedly; he'll soon become resentful. Instead, go back to basics and master the simple maneuvers first. Then approach the gate and combine the basic maneuvers as you attempt to open and close it. Each attempt will reveal if a basic maneuver needs work in your next schooling session.

# HAULING YOUR HORSE

**17**

SOONER or later, a horse owner wants or needs to haul his horse. Sometimes a friend with a trailer doesn't mind making the occasional trip to the veterinarian's office, or having you and your horse along as he travels to a nearby show, clinic, or trail ride. But you probably have plans for a truck and trailer of your own.

## The Trailer

Shop for a trailer as carefully as you shop for your vehicle. Your safety and that of your horse depends on it. Once safety has been ensured, consider all the trailer add-ons and extras you like. You can choose from many, some of which add to a horse's hauling comfort, and others that provide more for the owner's convenience.

Stock trailers generally have slatted sides and are sometimes referred to as cattle trailers. Some have rag-tops, as they're called, that can be fastened over the trailer's overhead framework, or the top can be metal. An enclosed trailer describes what most think of as a horse trailer, complete with a permanent top and solid sides. A combination trailer is a hybrid of the two, with the sides featuring both solid and slatted portions.

Bumper-pull trailers are most often two-horse trailers, although there are one-

*When your horse loads well and you're comfortable driving a vehicle pulling a trailer, a world of new riding experiences opens to you.*

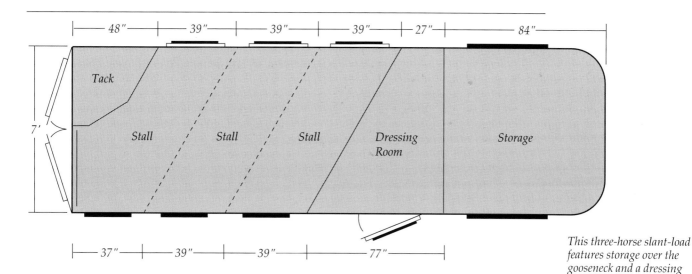

This three-horse slant-load features storage over the gooseneck and a dressing room. Tack storage is in a rear corner of the trailer.

horse, or single-shot, trailers on the market. Two-horse side-by-side trailers, with the horses hauled abreast, are most common, but two-horse slant-loads can also be purchased. Such trailers can be pulled with either a car or a truck providing the tow vehicle is substantial and powerful enough to handle the load.

A gooseneck trailer is so-named because of the hitch's appearance, which makes it possible to balance the load over the back axle of a truck. Goosenecks are available in a host of sizes for hauling from two to six horses, or even more. Such trailers often feature dressing rooms and tack compartments or can have self-contained living quarters. Gooseneck trailers can be straight-loads or slant-loads, where the horses are hauled at an angle across the bed of the trailer, which enables them to balance better during stops and starts.

The trailer hauling compartment—in length, height, and width—should be large enough that your horse can stand comfortably with room to spare. Guidelines from the *Horse Industry Handbook* recommend a trailer 10 inches taller than the "normal resting position" of a horse's head. Many trailers are about 6½ feet in height, but taller ones aren't unusual. Each stall in a two-horse side-by-side should be about 30 inches. The stall should have additional length, too, so a horse can better brace himself during the haul.

The butt-bar or chain keeps a horse from balancing his weight on the trailer door, which can weaken it. Too, should the door open unexpectedly, a butt-bar can keep your horse from being injured. Don't attempt to give your horse a few inches more room by not hooking the bar or chain.

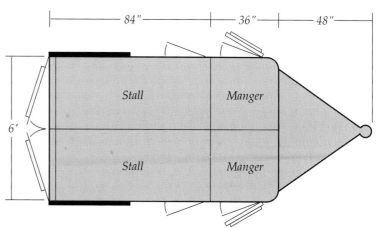

A typical two-horse bumper-pull trailer. Tack storage is under the mangers, and an escape door is provided in each stall.

**Illustrations courtesy of Sooner Trailer Manufacturing Co. Inc.**

Dealerships can supply the stall measurements for their trailers, which vary somewhat with the design. There are many options from which to choose. It's up to you to match the size of the hauling compartment with the size of your mount. But remember that the larger the space, the happier most horses will be. Cramming a horse into a too-small trailer can soon make him fretful, fighting the trailer or refusing to load.

Give some thought to the size of your budget before you start your search. There are many serviceable used trailers for sale that are well worth the money, but again the buyer must beware. Since used trailers are not as well-advertised as new ones, let

*Trailer designs can provide maximum tack storage in a minimum amount of floor space.*

check the flooring, especially along the sides and at the rear where urine tends to pool. Appearances can be deceiving, and what seems substantial on the surface may be rotten underneath. It is important that the cross-members under the flooring are well-spaced to provide adequate support. Eighteen inches should be the maximum, and less is better.

Replacing trailer flooring isn't that difficult a job, but does require some time. Treated oak is often used for flooring repairs since it lasts longer than untreated or softer woods. Leaving a small space between the boards is a good idea; urine can drain through the cracks.

Remember, too, that urine can make flooring slick, so use bedding, shavings for example, to absorb the moisture. Rubber mats also can help reduce slippage and cushion the ride for a horse as well. Mats should be heavy and well-fitted so a horse won't get them wadded under his feet during the haul. Remove mats and bedding periodically, when you clean the trailer, to allow the flooring to dry completely.

2/ *Brakes.* Trailers usually come equipped with electric brakes, which can be a real lifesaver when making an unexpected stop where the trailer might jack-knife. You'll make fewer repairs if the brake wiring is run through a conduit; exposed wiring can be easily broken or torn loose, particularly if you drive across an unmowed pasture.

3/ *Lights.* Running lights are required on trailers; it's the law, but maintaining properly working trailer lights is an ongoing chore. As with the brake system, the more of the lighting system exposed to the elements, the more repairs you make. Too, horses tied to trailers have been known to break lights and pull wiring loose, so consider the system design with that in mind.

4/ *Ventilation.* Your horse needs fresh air in a trailer, just as you do in the truck. If you're planning to buy an enclosed trailer, check to see that it's well-ventilated, preferably with adjustments so you can control the air flow and its direction.

5/ *Access.* The more you have access to your horse when he's loaded, the better. During routine hauling, you can check him more thoroughly without unloading,

your riding companions, farrier, or veterinarian know you're looking for one. Also check with new-trailer dealers who often have accepted used ones as trade-ins.

No matter how plain or fancy, large or small a trailer may be, safety is of primary importance when you haul your horse. Here are some things to consider.

1/ *Flooring.* Good flooring in your trailer is critical. Manure and urine contribute greatly to flooring decay, so clean the trailer after each use. Periodically

or offer him feed or water. Too, it's important that you have an escape route should you need one, should you be in a trailer with a horse, for whatever reason. Don't put yourself in a position to be trapped in a trailer. Of course, in an emergency situation, the more access you have, the quicker you can get to your horse.

## The Tow Vehicle

Your safety depends on how adequately a tow vehicle can handle the load of a trailer, so don't cut corners here. Many vehicles have optional towing packages that enhance suspension and stability, as well as cooling and wiring systems, and such. Too, dealerships have information and charts available that can help you match a vehicle's weight and size to the load. Considerations include the following:

1/ *Gross Combined Vehicle Weight.* The weight of the vehicle, the trailer and its load, and the passengers and any cargo is totaled to determine gross combined vehicle weight. Knowing this enables you to determine the engine size and the gear ratio needed to best handle the load.

2/ *Engine Size.* Evaluating engine size is sometimes confusing since they can be described by cubic inches, metric liters, or the number of cylinders. Define engine sizes by a common denominator. Then you can more easily compare them and determine the best value for towing the gross combined vehicle weight of your load in your terrain.

3/ *Gear Ratio.* This describes how many revolutions it takes to turn the rear axle. The higher the gear ratio, the more revolutions per minute, and the poorer the fuel economy, but the easier it is to pull the load. Again, check dealership information to find out what gear ratio is recommended for the load and engine size you are considering.

4/ *Hitch.* The trailer hitch, whether it's for a bumper-pull or gooseneck trailer, should be well-attached to the frame of the tow vehicle, and the ball properly sized for the trailer. Check your hitch regularly and make sure the ball is tight. Safety chains are required by law in some states.

*When purchasing a trailer, consider your horse's safety and comfort first, then consider options for your convenience.*

The height of the hitch is also a consideration, particularly with a bumper-pull trailer. Ideally, the trailer, when hooked up and loaded, should be level; this gives your horse a better ride.

## Loading Up

Loading a horse in a trailer is about as unnatural to a horse as backing him into territory he can't see. Consider the trailer from a horse's point of view, which is somewhat limited in this case. Remember

147

reading that his vision is not so great directly in front of and below his head? Yet, he is asked to step into that area, and even worse, tolerate some motion and unfamiliar footing underneath when he does. In addition, the trailer with its darker interior seems much like a cave to a horse. The average horse's inherent instincts come to the fore; he's sure that predators lie in wait there. It's no wonder some horses are difficult to load.

Now consider what you've learned about how a horse reacts when he faces the unknown. It's usually with flight or fight. And, if he has been mishandled during previous loading experiences, or if the driver was careless during a previous haul, the horse has had plenty of reinforcement to convince him that the trailer is a bad place to be.

A good horseman works to make trailer loading and hauling as comfortable an experience as possible, for both himself and his horse. And, yes, even a horse well-broke to load occasionally tries the best horseman as they approach the trailer door. So don't be surprised if your first horse, the one who loaded so well when you checked him out for purchase, challenges you the first time or two you load him. Be firm with him in this case; he's just checking to see if you're still the boss under those circumstances.

How do you make loading in a trailer a comfortable experience for a horse?

First and foremost, don't wait until you have to load a horse for the two of you to get trailer-loading experience. Allow yourself plenty of time for practice, then use it. Rushing the process only adds to a horse's initial uneasiness about loading.

Remember, you can't muscle him into a trailer, but you can teach him to load well by properly reinforcing the right response when a horse makes it.

The trailer should be hooked to the tow vehicle so the trailer doesn't roll just as the horse steps into it. It's also a good idea to use protective hauling wraps on a horse. A horse sometimes bumps his front cannon bones on the end of the trailer when loading, and can scrape his hind legs when exiting. Wraps can help ensure such scrapes or bruises aren't serious ones.

Many horses load better in a stock trailer with slatted sides that allows for improved vision and air circulation; the horse feels less likely to be trapped by predators. If the trailer is enclosed, open the front windows for more light. Some horses load more easily when they think they can see a way out. It sometimes helps, too, if a herd mate, who is comfortable inside a trailer, is awaiting your horse's arrival. When you load a horse, reinforce the idea that the trailer is a good place to be; rub him on the rump and have some hay or a handful of grain in the manger.

As you become familiar with the loading process, swap sides with the horse and vary his hauling position. Try him in a partially enclosed combination trailer, a fully enclosed one, or a slant-load.

More important, once you get a horse loaded, be aware that he's back there as you drive. Avoid quick starts and stops and fast turns that will leave him struggling to maintain his balance.

Never try to ride a horse into a trailer; that's asking for trouble. And, once you reach your destination and have unloaded a horse, fasten the trailer door securely. Occasionally a horse at an equine event gets loose or runs away with a child. Shutting the door eliminates him considering your trailer a possible escape route.

Before you approach the trailer to load your horse, do your homework. Be sure the path is free of obstacles and that the trailer door won't shut unexpectedly, startling the horse.

Here's where the time you've spent teaching your horse to move forward,

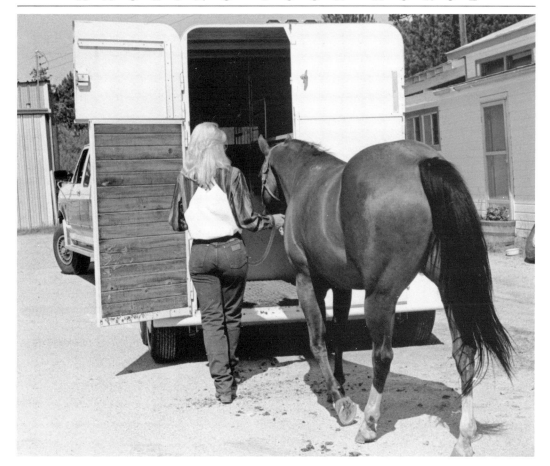

1/ This horse loads well, even in an enclosed two-horse trailer. Notice that both the upper and lower portions of the door are opened wide. If necessary, prop the doors open or have someone hold them, to prevent them from falling closed or bumping the horse as he loads into the trailer.

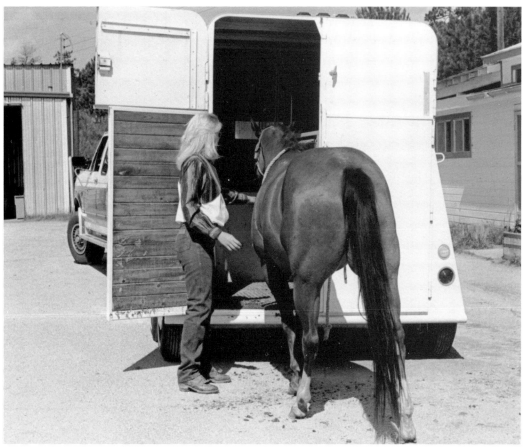

2/ The horse moves past the handler and into the trailer at her signal, much the same as that used to drive a horse forward when he is on a longe line.

3/ *The handler gives a reassuring pat as the horse steps in.*

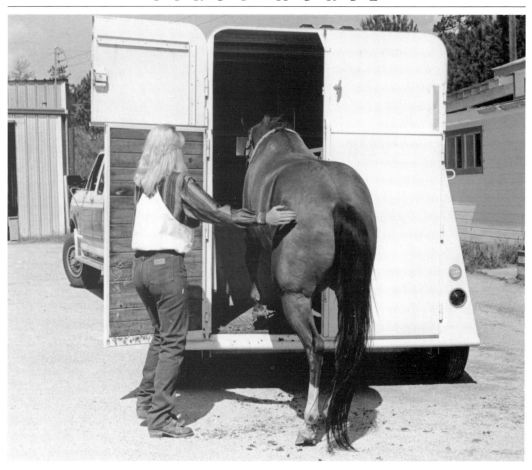

4/ *When securing the butt-bar, always stand to one side for safety in case the horse kicks or suddenly starts backing out before the butt-bar is fastened.*

when you cluck and motion behind him on the longe line, pays a bonus. In fact, it's best to take a few minutes, prior to loading, for ground work, to ensure you have a horse's attention and respect. If he doesn't respond as well as you would like, take a few minutes more to sharpen his response to your cues before you approach the trailer.

Not all horses who lead well will load well. Think about it. When being led properly, a horse is disciplined if he gets out of position and tries to work ahead of his handler. But when a horse loads well, he must move past the handler on cue, stepping ahead of him and into the trailer. The handler cues the horse to enter the trailer in much the same way he drives a horse forward on a longe line. A well-schooled horse can discern the difference in cues for leading or loading. The more you reinforce the right response to such cues before attempting to load a horse, the greater your chances for getting the job done easily.

Start a little distance from the trailer when you approach the trailer, to ensure that the horse's body is straight as you aim him—not yourself—directly at the compartment you want him to enter. Lead the horse in a matter-of-fact manner to the end of the trailer. As his head nears the end of the trailer, cue him to go past you and enter the trailer by motioning him forward with your right hand, stepping a little toward his hindquarters, if necessary.

Some people throw the lead rope over a horse's neck as he steps into the trailer; others prefer to drape the excess lead over the neck and use only one hand on the lead during the approach. It's your call; do whatever you feel comfortable with.

As soon as the horse is in the trailer, fasten the butt-chain or bar. If you need to, put your hand on the horse's rump to push him forward a step so you can fasten the chain. This is also a good time to rub him on the rump and praise him for making the right response.

Should you tie a horse in the trailer? That's up to you. In trailers with suitable partitions, many experienced horses haul fine without being tied. An inexperienced horse, however, can sometimes get his head down between his front legs in the trailer, unless he's tied.

If you tie your horse in the trailer, be sure to allow enough slack for him to lean back comfortably, to brace against the butt-bar before he takes the slack out of the tie rope. A horse will sometimes panic in a trailer, expecially in a side-by-side, when he finds he's tied short. But he won't if he can push against the butt-bar before the tie rope stretches tight.

If your trailer is equipped with ties, be sure they are long enough for a horse to easily maintain his balance. It's also a good idea to use quick-release snaps, either on the trailer ties or on lead ropes. Always use a quick-release knot, so you can free a horse's head quickly, if necessary. Always untie a horse before opening the trailer door and unfastening the butt-bar; otherwise a horse could wind up half-in and half-out of the trailer and risk injury.

Don't rush a horse when loading or unloading him. Let him take things at his own speed. Some well-schooled horses step quickly in or out of a trailer, totally confident that the handler won't put them in a bad situation. Other horses enter a trailer more slowly or exit it more cautiously, not entirely sure of procedure or of the handler. Remember: Each time you load a horse, he will either become a better-loading horse, or a worse one, but he never stays the same.

If you have a problem loader, or a horse not yet trained to load, it could be well worth your time to attend a clinic, read a book, or watch a training tape before you work with the horse. Mike Kevil's chapter on trailer loading in the *Western Horseman* book *Starting Colts* provides good information for teaching a horse to load.

# FEEDING YOUR HORSE

## 18

UNDERSTANDING a horse's nutritional requirements better enables you to maintain your horse's good physical condition, usually with fewer digestive upsets for him and at a more reasonable cost to you. Why pay for tasty extras or excess feed when you may not need either to keep your horse fit and healthy.

A word of caution here: Fit and healthy doesn't mean overfat and full of energy.

First-time owners often buy the right kind of first horse—a broke horse, who likely has been fed correctly for the amount of exercise he has been getting. The first-time owner may not be able to ride as regularly, or perhaps can't turn the

horse out of a stall as often. But the new owner continues to feed as if the horse was still receiving the same, regular exercise. And the owner sometimes even feeds a little extra grain or another flake of hay, just to give his new horse something to do in the stall.

The end result? One of two things, or both, usually happens to that great first horse. 1/ His energy level becomes so high that it's inappropriate, or even unsafe, for a novice owner to deal with while learning to ride, or 2/ the horse becomes overfat and physically unfit. Then, when the new owner is able to spend a weekend riding, the horse natu-

*This tire has been recycled into a hay feeder.*

rally becomes sore-muscled and, consequently, cranky to ride, resistant even to simple commands.

## Feeding Considerations

Developing good judgment when feeding a horse is as important to your riding program as learning when and how to reinforce a rein cue. Here are some basic considerations, no matter what specific rations you choose.

1/ Nature's plan for the horse, for hundreds of years, determined that he was a grazing, herbivorous animal, and that remains part of the horse today. He needs roughage, whether it is eaten directly from a growing pasture or from baled hay, for the digestive process. He can, in fact, subsist on roughage alone providing he is mature, his work load isn't too heavy, and the quality of the roughage is sufficient.

2/ Because the horse wandered and grazed throughout the day, as he evolved, his stomach developed somewhat small in relation to his body mass. His digestive tract fares better, even today, when he eats smaller amounts more often. This is particularly important if a horse isn't on pasture and able to graze throughout the day.

3/ Maintain regular feeding hours as best you can. This isn't as critical with a pastured horse, who will have a continuous supply of roughage in his digestive tract, as it is with a stabled one who must rely on your punctuality to ensure good digestion. If you happen to miss a feeding, don't double the ration next time. Overfeeding is uncomfortable and unsafe for a horse.

4/ When planning a feed ration, consider a horse's age, size, and use. A 1,000-pound mature gelding, for example, who is ridden hard 5 days weekly has different nutritional requirements than a small pony ridden lightly on the weekends.

5/ Measure feed by weight, not by volume. A 3-pound coffee can full of oats won't weigh the same as one full of corn or pellets. Nor will a flake of grass hay likely weigh as much as a comparable sized flake of alfalfa.

6/ Be as consistent in your feeding program as possible, always taking a horse's current condition and exercise regimen into consideration. Rule of thumb: Increase the grain as the workload increases, and as the work decreases,

*Feed by weight, not by volume.*

decrease the grain proportionately, always being sure your horse has roughage in his daily diet.

7/ If you must change a horse's ration, do so gradually during several feedings. Quick changes in ration can result in colic, which, for a horse, can be life-threatening.

8/ Allow a horse time to digest his ration before working him hard. If you must work him, feed only a portion of his ration beforehand.

9/ Don't, however, feed the remaining portion of the ration to a hot horse. Cool out the horse first.

10/ Keep the hay manger and grain box clean at all times. Remove old feed from the trough, and try to determine why the horse refused the feed. Was the ration too large, or was the feed dusty or moldy?

11/ If your horse seems to be a sloppy eater who drops or wastes much of his grain, check his teeth. Perhaps a veterinar-

*Unloading and stacking hay are never easy; this set-up makes the chore about as easy as it gets. The barn aisle has ample room for the truck and trailer, so the hay can be stacked right in the barn, out of the weather and convenient for feeding.*

ian needs to float them so the horse can better utilize his grain.

12/ Check a horse's droppings, too, to help determine how well he is utilizing his feed or if internal parasites are present. Take note of any change in the consistency or color of the manure.

13/ If your horse tends to bolt his food down, put bricks or rocks, so large that he can't swallow them, in the trough with the feed. The horse will be forced to slow down and eat around the objects.

14/ Plenty of clean, fresh water goes hand-in-hand with a good feeding program. A mature horse can drink from 10 to 12 gallons daily, or even more in extreme temperature. Some people prefer using automatic waterers. These are convenient, but make it impossible to monitor a horse's daily water intake. Other horsemen prefer using buckets, since they can tell that a horse is drinking normally and getting enough water to meet his needs.

15/ A horse also needs salt in his daily diet, whether it is found in a commercial mixed feed or provided free-choice from a salt block. With heavy work and/or in extreme temperatures, a horse may need more salt than is provided in commercial feed.

# Roughage

Roughage provides higher fiber in a horse's diet than grains or concentrates and is necessary for his digestive well-being. Ideally, a horse would have acres of good pasture from which to pick and choose the most succulent of grasses. Providing pasture is well-maintained and fertilized, it may suffice to maintain an idle horse. The American Horse Council's *Horse Industry Handbook* recommends a stocking rate of one horse per 2 acres of pasture to provide substantial nutrients, but that rate varies widely from one region to the next, depending on the climate, rainfall, and soil type.

If fewer acres of pasture are available, perhaps the horse can be turned out only a few hours daily, or rotated from one small pasture to another every few weeks to prevent overgrazing and to help control the internal parasites that thrive in sparse, overpopulated pastures. If, on the other hand, pasture is coarsely overgrown, it can be mowed to encourage fresh growth, which is more palatable to horses.

Do remember that with a stalled horse, who has had only hay, it is better to increase his grazing time gradually when turning him out on fresh, spring grass. This will help avoid digestive upsets.

Unfortunately, having acres of pasture available isn't always a realistic option for horse owners nowadays. Often a horse has only a dry lot or a run available, so an owner must substitute baled hay to satisfy the horse's need for roughage, or dehydrated forage that has been pelleted or cubed.

Hay, the most commonly used forage, generally falls into one of two categories—grass or legume. Grass hay is often considered higher in fiber than legume hay, which usually is higher in protein. Because of this, legume hay such as alfalfa is often more expensive to buy than grass hay. Common grass hays include Bermuda, timothy, brome, orchard grass, bahia, and others. Many horsemen prefer mixed hay, a combination of grass and legume hays, since they feel it offers a balance of fiber and protein in the roughage. The best hay, as far as most horsemen are concerned, is one that is available locally because it will be less expensive to purchase and the delivery charges will be less. The catch? The hay grower must be reliable—both in providing a sufficient quantity of hay and in routinely baling quality hay. The variety of hay that grows best in an area varies regionally, again depending on climate and soil conditions. Check with horsemen you know or call your county extension agent to determine a good local hay to feed and for help in finding a reliable supplier.

Many factors affect the quality of hay—its stage of maturity at cutting, the growing season, the soil type, fertilizer applications, and such. So it's hard to accurately evaluate the nutritional value in hay. Forage tests can be run on hay, but the results apply only to that particular cutting of hay, in that particular field, and at that particular time.

There are, however, some guidelines for assessing hay and feeding it to your horse. Remember, the better the quality of forage you provide your horse, the less grain will be required to keep him in good physical condition.

1/ Hay should have good color in the bale—green. Alfalfa hay in the bale is usually a deeper green than most grass hays. A tan or brown color throughout a bale can indicate that the hay was rained on in the field, after being cut but prior to baling. If that's the case, the nutrient value will be less.

However, a bale could be sun-bleached on the outside edges and green inside, which could indicate that the bale sat in the field or on a truck, prior to being stored. This bale is not as eye-appealing as one moved promptly from the field to storage, but probably hasn't lost much nutritional value.

2/ The stems in the hay should be somewhat fine since immature hay works better in a horse's digestive tract than does more mature hay full of coarse stems.

3/ When purchasing hay, such as alfalfa, for example, evaluate the leafiness of the hay. The more leaves in comparison to the stem, the more digestible the hay usually, and this indicates that the hay wasn't too mature when baled. Many nutrients are in the leaves.

4/ Hay should be baled at an appropriate moisture content. When baled too dry, alfalfa leaves, for instance, tend to shatter off the stem, leaving a horse with more stem and less nutritional value.

Any hay baled with too high a moisture content is subject to mold. This creates digestive problems for your horse. When you open a bale, always look for bluish spots that could indicate mold and smell the hay for mold's distinctive odor. Hay baled with a too-high moisture content is also subject to spontaneous combustion.

5/ Always break open a bale before feeding and check it for foreign matter. Then loosen the flake even more as you place it in the manger, keeping a sharp eye out. Tree limbs caught in the hay bale, for example, are not such a great problem; most horses simply shove them aside and eat around them. But wire, metal objects, or dead animals, which sometimes can cause botulism, baled into hay can create problems for your horse, as can blister beetles.

Usually found in alfalfa hay grown in western states, particularly Texas or Oklahoma, blister beetles are very toxic to horses. The risk from blister beetles is usually less in first-cutting alfalfa or in a fall cutting. Few other insects found in baled hay are harmful to horses. But if you are uncertain about anything you find in a

155

*If necessary, hay can be stored outside, on pallets and tarped down. Although the lower portion of this stack will be somewhat bleached by the sun, the tarp on top will help prevent moisture from getting into the stack, which could result in moldy hay.*

*Hay cubes are easier to handle and store than baled hay.*

your hay, don't feed from that bale until you identify the problem.

6/ Small, rectangular bales, weighing from 50 to 75 pounds each, are common because they are easier to handle and store. It is important to store hay properly—on a dry surface and either in a barn or under a cover of some sort—to maintain as much nutritional value as possible. Hay is highly flammable and, consequently, a fire hazard, and it should always be handled as such.

7/ Rule of thumb: Feed about 1 percent of a horse's body weight in roughage for

daily maintenance. A 1,000-pound horse would require about 10 pounds of hay per day. Another way of putting the same rule of thumb: Feed 1 pound of roughage per day for every 100 pounds of body weight. A horse's needs vary depending on his amount of daily work and the quality of the hay. Pregnant mares or growing young horses, for example, will have greater forage needs than an idle mature horse.

8/ Roughage alternatives to grass or legume hay include hay that has been pelleted or cubed. Pelleted hay is finer than cubed hay. Consequently, a horse receiving only pellets might experience digestive disorders; his system may require more coarse roughage than the pellets provide. In addition, a horse can eat pellets faster than he can hay, so a stalled horse may become bored more quickly without the longer feeding period to occupy his time. As a result of boredom, a horse can develop vices such as cribbing or wood-chewing.

Hay cubes are larger, about 1½ to 2 inches, and coarser than pellets. Cubed hay, too, is often made from alfalfa, and like the pelleted hay, is easier to handle and store than baled hay. You must weigh the increased cost of pellets and cubes against the convenience they provide to decide if either is a suitable alternative for you. However, many horsemen believe that it is more natural for a horse to eat hay than pellets or cubes.

*Garbage containers with lids that fasten tightly are excellent for grain storage.*

# Feeding Grain

Although forage is the place to start planning your feeding program, grain provides more energy for a horse working hard on a daily basis. There are a host of considerations when selecting a grain ration to supplement a horse's daily forage. Fiber, protein, and energy, along with vitamins and minerals, are all needed, and must be balanced properly to meet a horse's nutritional needs.

Being exact in a feeding program is a science in and of itself, one about which volumes have been written. Mastering precise equine nutrition would, no doubt, leave you little spare time in which to ride. However, you can still feed your horse well and ride him, too. Feed companies study equine nutrition for you, trying to make their products easy for you to use.

You also can ask your county extension agent for help with a feed ration analysis. He can lead you through the process or provide you with the feeding information available in your state's 4-H horse project manual. Ask, too, to be notified when your county extension service offers any feeding or nutrition seminars. As always, you can rely on the best horseman you know to help you plan a feeding program.

No matter how you supplement your horse's forage, there's some basic information about feeds and equine nutrition you need to know.

1/ To meet nutritional requirements and for supplemental energy, you can feed your horse a grain, such as oats or corn, a grain mixture, a complete feed, or a balanced feed. Complete feeds include extra fiber for roughage and should be adequate to maintain a horse, along with a good supply of fresh water, but such feeds are usually more expensive. Some feeds are balanced with specific purposes in mind—growing a colt out well, maintaining a mature horse, sustaining a pregnant mare, etc.

2/ The feed bag label should include a guaranteed analysis of the feed and list the percentages of protein, fat, and fiber. A complete feed, for example, has a higher fiber content, and a feed high in fat can create more energy without adding bulk.

3/ Feed labels also list ingredients, but beware of generic terms, such as grain by-products. That may include anything— wheat, corn, oats, etc.

4/ TDN is an acronym for total digestible nutrients. Though not always

**These rules of thumb are merely a starting point in determining a horse's ration.**

*Pelleted feed is less bulky than extruded feed, which looks somewhat like dog food.*

*Oats have long been considered a staple in the equine diet.*

Crimping is a similar process and is often used on oats. Corn, however, can be cracked and often is labeled as such.

Ground feeds can be pelleted, which reduces the feed bulk and dust in a ration. Horses sometimes are finicky eaters, so having required nutrients pelleted with the ground feed is beneficial; a horse is less likely to refuse to eat the less palatable, but necessary, part of his ration. Extruded feed, also made from ground feed, looks more like dry dog food, but weighs less than an equal volume of pelleted feed. Since a horse can't bolt extruded feed as quickly as pellets, the extruded feed can be better for a fast eater, reducing the chance of a bellyache.

6/ As with roughages, grains should be fed by weight, not volume. A small scale is almost a necessity in the feed room. Too, an adequate grain ration, for a moderately ridden horse also receiving good forage, seems small to the human eye, in relation to the horse's size. So weighing the ration helps prevent overfeeding.

7/ How much grain should you feed? A good starting point is to use the same rule of thumb that you use in feeding forage—a pound of grain per 100 pounds of body weight, or about 1 percent of the body weight—for a horse who is getting regular exercise. For example, a 1,000-pound, mature horse, exercised daily, would need about 10 pounds of roughage a day and about 10 pounds of supplemental feed, preferably dispersed in two or three feedings over a 24-hour period. If the horse isn't being ridden daily, he won't need as much grain, just as he won't if the roughage he's receiving is higher in quality.

These rules of thumb are merely a starting point in determining a horse's ration. Inexpensive tapes are available for measuring a horse's barrel to determine his approximate weight, and an inexpensive scale is a must in the feed room. Use both to eliminate guesswork by weighing the horse and the feed. Then make adjustments for the forage quality and the amount of exercise your horse receives.

Another consideration in figuring rations: Some horses are considered "easy keepers." In other words, they seem to maintain good body condition with less effort than a "hard keeper" who, perhaps, is more discriminating in his tastes, or finicky in his eating habits. Again, learn from your first horse. He will show you if

found on a feed label, TDN is a consideration in any ration since it is one of the building blocks in a good ration. The others are proteins, minerals, and vitamins. Just as with people, horses need a well-balanced ration for good health. Different feeds provide varying amounts of the nutritional building blocks.

5/ Feed grains are processed in different ways. A ground feed is often fine in texture although a coarse one is better for horses. Rolling a grain, such as oats, changes the texture by breaking the kernel of the grain.

he's an easy keeper or a hard one, and you will learn how to accommodate that in your feeding program.

8/ Oats, whether whole, rolled, or crimped, long have been the traditional grain of choice for most horsemen. Oats have more fiber than most grains, which is good for a horse's digestive tract. For this reason, oats are considered safer to feed since they allow a greater margin for feeding error than does a more concentrated feed, for example. However, oats can vary greatly in quality from one bag to the next. Too, oats are somewhat lower in digestible energy than corn, for example.

9/ Corn also can be fed in a variety of ways—whole, shelled, cracked, or rolled. Since corn is much higher in digestible energy, it must be fed carefully; otherwise your horse's energy level may become difficult to deal with.

10/ Barley is another grain often fed to horses. But the hull is tougher than an oat hull, so the barley must be rolled or crimped.

11/ Commercial feeds include a mixture of corn, oats, and other grains, and may have soybean meal to provide more protein, wheat bran, vitamins, and minerals added. Many commercial feeds are called "sweet" feeds since molasses is often added to the blend to reduce dust and make the feed tastier. Some sweet feeds are drier and less sticky than others. Due to a different manufacturing process, a pelleted complete feed is dry, as are extruded feeds, but both are costlier than other feeds.

12/ Trace mineralized salt, although added to most commercial feeds, may not be sufficient to meet a horse's requirements, which vary with the work load, a horse's maturity, extreme temperatures, etc. Small salt bricks can be placed in a stall feeder or in a special holder fastened to the stall wall. Much larger salt blocks are available for use in the pasture.

13/ There are a multitude of feed supplements on the market today, formulated to improve everything from a horse's haircoat to hoof growth, along with a host of multivitamin and mineral supplements. For the average mature horse, ridden moderately, a well-balanced ration of good forage and grain should suffice, along with a salt block. However, a pregnant mare, a growing colt, or an old pensioner might well need additions to their rations.

*Commercially prepared mixed feeds include corn and oats and often have other ingredients, such as wheat bran, added.*

*Salt blocks are suitable for use in the pasture. Holders for the smaller bricks can be fastened to stall walls.*

If you are using your first horse hard, riding him many hours daily, a feed supplement might well be in order. When you add a supplement to your horse's ration, have a good reason for doing so. For example, when his haircoat doesn't look so great in the spring and you plan to show him, supplementing his ration may help gain the desired coat condition faster. Supplements, however, are often expensive to use and should never be considered a replacement for a well-balanced ration of forage and feed.

# HEALTH CARE FOR YOUR HORSE

**19**

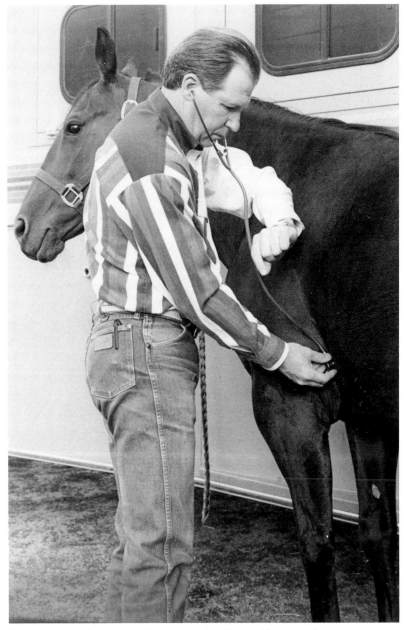

*Checking a horse's pulse rate is fairly simple with or without a stethoscope.*

ANOTHER important aspect of good horsemanship is health care management. When your horse is ill or injured, you can't enjoy riding him. Too, the purchase of a horse usually represents an investment of sorts, so it makes sense to protect your investment. Besides, you don't want to see a horse distressed by poor health. A good horseman gives timely vaccinations and deworming medications.

Learning the normal vital signs for your horse when he's healthy is one of the easiest ways to recognize when he isn't. That knowledge, along with a few basic medical supplies can help ensure your horse's good health.

Several measures already discussed, such as a good feeding program, maintaining a clean environment, and providing regular exercise, help keep a horse more fit or help minimize his risk for illness or injury. The key to making any preventive measure work in favor of your horse's continuing good health is to use it on a regular, ongoing basis.

## Vaccinations

Although some vaccinations are recommended for horses nationwide, others are necessary only in certain geographic regions. However, horsemen have become increasingly mobile in recent years, hauling their horses more often to many events and activities, which can contribute to the spread of disease. A local veterinarian is your best source of guidance for planning immunizations. He can recommend a program for your horse, appropriate for your location and your riding plans.

Whatever the vaccination program you use, carry it out methodically, following up with boosters whenever necessary to build your horse's immunity to the highest level possible. Most people vaccinate regularly in the spring, prior to heavy insect infestation and more frequent contact with other horses at equine events. Some vaccines are recommended for use more often than others, depending on how frequently you travel with a horse, subjecting him to a higher risk for disease.

Here are some common equine vaccinations and a little information about the diseases they help protect your horse against. Consult an equine health-care professional for more information.

1/ Tetanus, or lockjaw, is a problem for horses just as it is with people. Horses, like people, suffer wounds that invite the disease, caused by bacteria. Understand that, no matter how hard you work at maintaining a safe environment for your horse, it's likely you will have to deal with a serious cut or puncture wound at some time. Tetanus is a serious disease and can be fatal. Your horse should be vaccinated and given a booster annually and also in case of injury. Tetanus toxoid vaccines provide long-lasting immunity. Another vaccine, tetanus antitoxin, gives immediate short-term protection and is used most when an injury occurs.

2/ Equine encephalomyelitis, commonly called sleeping sickness, is a virus transmitted by biting insects, usually mosquitoes. Sleeping sickness affects the nervous system and can cause paralysis or death in horses. There are eastern, western, and Venezuelan strains of the disease, but a vaccination is available to protect against each.

3/ Influenza is a viral respiratory disease in horses, just as it is in man. Although it isn't necessarily fatal to most horses, influenza can be deadly, for example, to an old or a very young horse, or any horse whose general health is poor. If you haul your horse a lot, where he experiences more stress and greater contact with other horses, your veterinarian may recommend that you vaccinate for influenza every 2 months or until the risk of exposure decreases.

4/ Respiratory rhinopneumonitis is likely of more importance to you than the form of the disease that causes abortion in pregnant mares. Both are caused by viruses. Respiratory rhino, as it's known, is seldom fatal, but is extremely contagious. Again, the more you travel with your horse, the more frequent his boosters should be.

5/ Strangles, or distemper, often occurs in highly stressed horses and is a bacterial infection. Because a horse's lymph nodes under his jaw swell, he is apt to find eating and drinking more difficult, hence the name "strangles." The bacteria is contagious and, like tetanus, can thrive in an area for several years. The vaccines available today are effective and easy to use.

6/ Rabies can affect a horse's nervous system, just as it does a dog's. By the time you figure out what the problem is, it's too late to do much about it. You can become infected with rabies as well. Your local veterinarian can help determine your horse's risk from rabies, which varies with wildlife populations from one region to the next.

7/ Potomac horse fever causes intestinal disorders and is sometimes fatal. Named for the Potomac River region where it was discovered, the disease is no longer limited to that area of the country. There isn't a great deal of information available about Potomac horse fever, but ticks are considered carriers of the disease. Again, consult a local veterinarian to determine if this disease is a threat in your area.

8/ Equine infectious anemia, or swamp fever, is a viral blood disease for which there is no vaccine and no cure. There is a test, however, that can determine if a horse is a carrier of the disease—a Coggins test. Coggins testing is required in many states and for interstate travel, often on an annual basis, but sometimes semiannually. EIA regulations vary from state to state. Horses determined to be carriers are placed under immediate quarantine. It is important that you request a current Coggins test on any horse you purchase; otherwise you place your entire barn at risk.

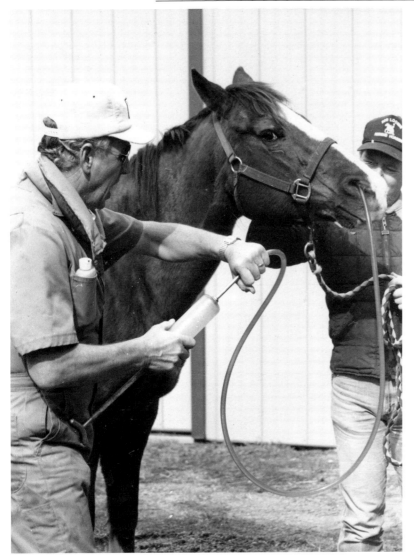

*For many years, tube-worming was the primary method for controlling internal parasites, but most horsemen wanted their veterinarians to do the job.*

## Internal Parasites

Internal parasites—worms—are an ever-present problem for horsemen. No matter how great the effort to control internal parasites, nearly all horses are affected by them. Unfortunately, it's hard to visually determine that a horse is wormy until the problem has become pronounced. So a good deworming program is important to your horse's health.

Here are some common outward indications that your horse is infected with internal parasites.

1/ A rough haircoat. This is particularly noticeable in the spring when a horse doesn't shed as quickly or as cleanly as he should.

2/ Rubbed-out tail hair. If your horse backs up to the fence to scratch his hindquarters frequently, he might be infested with worms. The missing tail hair results from the frequent rubbing.

3/ Unthriftiness in general. In other words, your horse's general appearance isn't as good as it should be for the amount of feed he's receiving; he seems to be a hard keeper. It's likely the nutrients in his feed are not going to his good health, but rather to support a host of parasites. However, a horse can have a good haircoat and be in good flesh, yet still be loaded with worms.

4/ Frequent colic, a chronic cough, or an anemic appearance. Each can result from parasite infestation. The focal point for some parasites is the digestive system. Other parasites affect a horse's circulatory system more, but any parasite presents a potential health problem.

5/ Fecal worms. By the time you can see worms in a horse's feces, your horse is host to many parasites. A veterinarian can test the feces at any time to determine what parasites are present and to what extent, whether you can actually see the worms or not.

There are four principal types of internal parasites found in horses: ascarids, strongyles, pinworms, and bots.

1/ Ascarids, or roundworms, most often affect young horses. By the time horses are considered grown, most of them usually develop an immunity to these large roundworms. When mature, roundworms can cause intestinal disorders such as colic. Roundworms have about a 3-month life cycle and develop when a horse ingests the eggs with his water or feed when grazing. A new supply of eggs, about 200,000 per day from one female worm, is spread in the horse's environment through his manure. These eggs are hardy and can live for long durations before finding another host horse, where the new crop matures inside the horse's body.

2/ Strongyles, more commonly called bloodworms, are found in horses of all ages, usually in the large intestine. These worms in the larvae stage, too, are durable, even in freezing temperatures although hot, dry conditions minimize their infestation in pastures. Different types of bloodworms can damage the liver, cause diarrhea or colic, or disrupt blood flow by causing arterial clotting.

3/ Pinworms develop in a horse's colon or rectum, once they have been ingested. Although pinworms don't cause severe damage to a horse, they lay eggs around the anus, which irritates the tail area and causes the horse to rub it excessively.

4/ Bots in a horse's stomach are actually the larvae of the bot fly, which lays eggs, usually, on a horse's leg hair. When a horse licks the hair with eggs, the tiny larvae burrow into his tongue and mouth. As the bot matures, he travels to the stomach lining where he spends the winter, before being passed from a horse's body and developing into a mature fly. In addition to using a good deworming program to reduce bot infestation, you can use a sharp knife or a special scraper to remove the yellowish eggs visible on the hair of a horse's leg.

A horseman's best recourse to control all forms of internal parasites is to deworm his horse regularly and keep stalls and runs as free of manure as possible. Dragging pastures, especially when it's hot and dry, breaks up manure and helps prevent larvae and eggs from thriving. Concentrating too many horses in too small an area is not a good management practice. As the amount of manure increases, so does the likelihood of parasite infestation. Nor is it a good practice to ground-feed horses, which makes it easier for horses to become reinfected with parasites. Use feeders and hay mangers if at all possible.

Many dewormers are on the market today. Some products are parasite-specific, formulated for a particular type worm. Other deworming agents are effective on all types of worms. However, any product must be used on a regular basis to successfully control internal parasites and break their life cycles. Plan a deworming program; then stick with it.

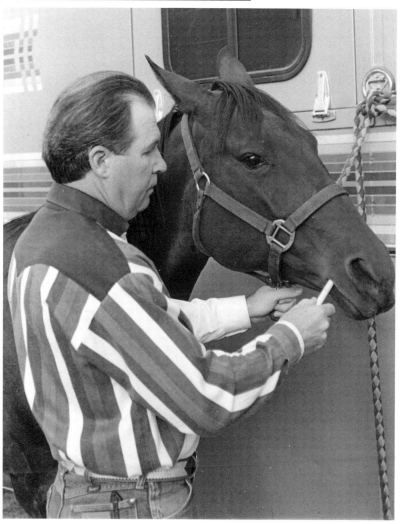

*The average horseman can safely administer the paste deworming agents on the market nowadays.*

Dewormers can be administered in several ways—by tubing, as a paste, or in the feed. Until recent years, a deworming program was not considered complete unless a stomach tube was used to deworm a horse each spring and fall. This usually required a veterinarian's expertise to get the job done safely. Nowadays a horseman can use an all-purpose, ivermectin-based dewormer, ideally about every 2 months. Or he can implement a continuous control program, mixing small doses of deworming agent in the daily feed ration. Either method makes controlling internal parasites a relatively easy task for anyone. As with feeding, the amount of dewormer used depends on the weight of your horse.

# Checking Your Horse

By knowing normal vital signs—pulse rate, respiration rate, and temperature—for your horse, you can more easily recognize the onset of potential health problems. Quicker detection means more immediate treatment. Too, a knowledge of normal vital signs, for comparison with those at the time of illness, is helpful information to pass along to a veterinarian treating a sick horse. It also helps to know what normal gut sounds and capillary refill time are for your horse and how to check for dehydration.

Since vital signs vary somewhat among horses, you must check your horse's normal standing rates, as they're known, when he is relaxed at home under ordinary, everyday circumstances. These normal rates become the basis for comparison whenever you think your horse is ill or in distress.

1/ Temperature for a mature horse can range from 99 to 101 degrees and still be considered normal, but a foal's temperature, on the average, is usually a little higher at 100 to 102 degrees. Take your horse's temperature a few times over a several-day period. Not only will the procedure become a routine one for you and the horse, you will get a more accurate idea of what constitutes a normal temperature for your horse.

Use a rectal thermometer to take a horse's temperature, holding it in place for at least 2 minutes to get an accurate reading. The thermometer should be lubricated with petroleum jelly before use, and cleaned with alcohol after each use. Take your time when approaching a horse to get a temperature reading, rubbing down his rump to relax him before inserting the thermometer. It's also wise to use a tail clip, or alligator clip, attached to the thermometer with a string, to prevent losing the thermometer in the rectum or dropping and breaking it.

2/ Normal pulse rate can range from about 30 or 40 beats a minute in a mature horse to as high as 60 to 80, which is about normal for a nursing foal. As with temperature, factors such as a horse's age or sex

*Normal temperature rates can vary somewhat from one horse to the next. Knowing what is normal for your horse helps you recognize a potential health problem quicker.*

Many horsemen choose to paste-worm because of the convenience. The premeasured paste guns, similar to large syringes, have clearly marked dosages and are easy to adjust. Anyone who has ever used his thumb on a horse's interdental space when bridling him can probably learn to use a paste gun effectively.

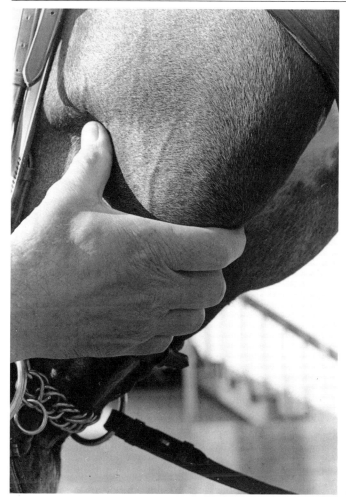

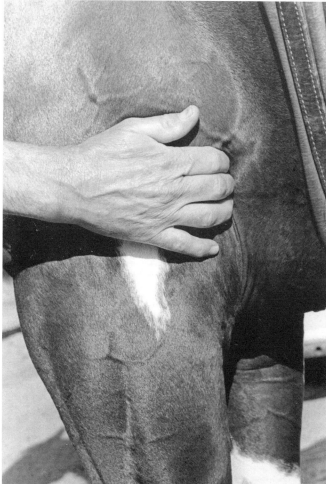

*A common place for checking a horse's pulse is under his jaw.*

*Here's another place used to check a horse's pulse. Some people can feel a pulse more easily on the lower leg, below the knee and along the cannon bone.*

or level of fitness, can affect the pulse rate, so it's important to determine the normal range for your particular horse.

Check the pulse rate anywhere a large artery runs near the surface of the horse's skin—under a horse's jaw, for example, or inside a horse's leg. Press lightly with your fingertips and feel for the regular, steady beat of the horse's heart. If you have difficulty, have your veterinarian show you how to find a pulse point.

Using a watch with a minute hand, count the beats per minute. You can shorten the process by counting the beats for 15 seconds and multiplying by four to get a 1-minute rate. Again, check your horse's pulse several times, when he's relaxed and comfortable, to ascertain his normal rate.

3/ Respiration rate reflects how regular and even a horse's breathing is. Many horsemen learn to evaluate a horse's breathing by studying the motion in the flank as the animal inhales and exhales, or by seeing how much the nostrils are distended when the horse takes a breath. Normal equine respiration rates vary from 10 to 20 breaths a minute when the animal is at rest.

An easy way to determine respiration rate is to hold the back of your hand near a horse's nostril. Again, using a watch,

within the normal range for that horse at the end of the 5-minute period, the animal has not been overstressed. If the rates are not normal, the animal obviously needs more fitting before being asked to exercise to that extent again.

This, of course, is a broad guideline, but helpful to know, particularly when a first horse is an older one. There is often concern about riding the older horse too hard, especially in extreme weather. Many children can master the techniques required to take pulse and respiration rates and, thus, can see immediately how their horses are affected by the amount of exercise.

4/ Capillary refill time is determined when you check your horse's mucous membranes, such as the linings of the mouth or nostrils. Healthy mucous membranes should be pink in color; a yellowish cast or a deep blue color indicates problems. Too, these membranes should be moist, otherwise dehydration could be the culprit.

Check capillary refill time when you check the mucous membranes in the mouth. Lift the horse's upper lip and press your finger or thumb against his gum. The result will be a white spot that should regain its color within 2 seconds. If the time required to refill the white spot with color is longer than 2 seconds, your horse has a problem. The longer the refill time, the more severe the problem usually is.

5/ Gut sounds can be checked with an inexpensive stethoscope, which can also be used to check his heartbeat. Although the heartbeat provides a consistent, rhythmic sound, a horse's gut, depending on where the stethoscope is placed, can produce a variety of sounds.

Only by routinely listening to your horse's gut can you learn what sounds are normal for different areas of his abdomen. Place the stethoscope on the side of the abdomen, then underneath, and listen to the differences. Or, give your horse a little grain, and listen to the gut sounds change. Keep in mind that you should almost always be able to hear gut sounds. If you suspect your horse has colic and you cannot hear any gut sounds, you should call your veterinarian.

6/ The dehydration pinch test is a simple one. Pinch the skin on the side of a horse's neck and hold it for a few seconds, then release the skin. If the folded skin quickly resumes its normal position, it's a

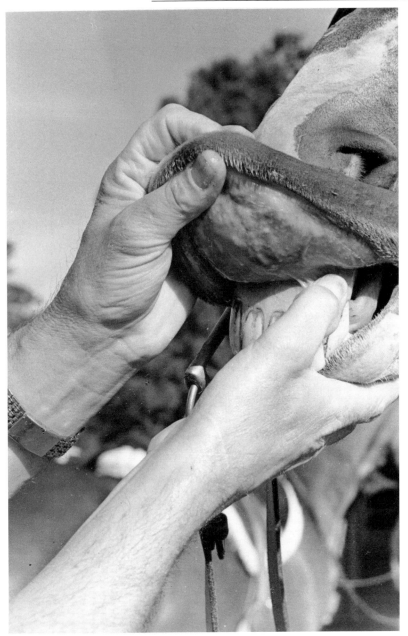

*Checking a horse's capillary refill time can give a quick indication of the severity of an equine health problem.*

count the number of times the horse exhales, blowing air across your hand, during a 1-minute period. Or count the breaths for 15 seconds and multiply by four to get a 1-minute respiration rate.

Pulse and respiration rates also are helpful to evaluate a horse's overall fitness or determine if a riding program is stressing the animal to his limits of endurance. A rider familiar with his mount's normal pulse and respiration rates can immediately check both following strenuous activity and, using his watch, begin a 5-minute countdown. If the rates are

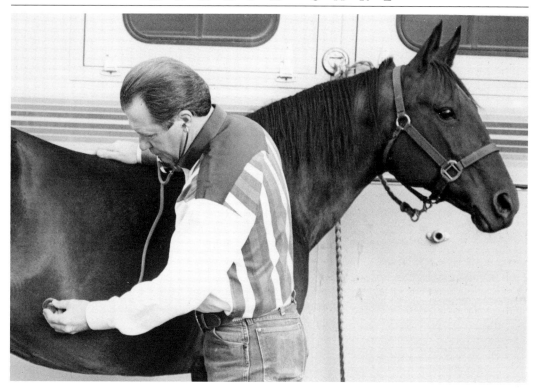

*Listen to a horse's gut sounds periodically, so you know what is normal. Note that the stethoscope is placed farther back along a horse's barrel to check gut sounds than it is when checking the heart rate.*

**Excessive exercise under extreme conditions often results in heat stroke.**

good sign. But, if the fold remains after about 3 seconds, your horse likely is dehydrated.

## Common Problems

The following are some of the more common equine health problems you're apt to experience with your horse.

1/ Colic is an intestinal tract disorder that can be caused, for example, by irregular feeding, stress, a change in feed, or internal parasites. Colic can take the form of mild intestinal spasms or a major blockage, or impaction, of the digestive tract. Or a horse can have a life-threatening "twisted gut," which occurs when the intestine is twisted abnormally and displaced. This is the most common disorder found in horses and potentially one of the most deadly.

A colicked horse usually appears restless and uneasy. He often paws with a front foot and/or tries to lie down and roll in an effort to relieve the pain in his abdomen. He may nuzzle his abdomen with his head or try to kick at it with his hind feet. Any or all of these signs, especially in excess, are a call to action since colic is somewhat unpredictable and quickly can result in a horse's death.

Contact a veterinarian immediately. In years past, a colicky horse was walked; it was feared that if he laid down, he might

roll and that would increase the odds of him twisting an intestine. Nowadays, that's not always the case, unless a horse is trying to violently roll. Do whatever the veterinarian recommends.

Colic is often treated with lubricants to soften the stool, anti-inflammatory drugs, or sedatives to relieve the pain. Many horsemen prefer to keep Banamine® or dipyrone on hand for pain relief, particularly for use with colic, but not everyone is comfortable with injecting the drugs. Paste medications can be administered orally, but are sometimes slower-acting than the injections. Any such drug should be used only under veterinary supervision. In extreme cases of colic, surgery may be indicated.

The best thing a horseman can do to help prevent colic is to use good judgment in his management practices by implementing a sensible feed program, controlling internal parasites, and providing adequate equine dental care to ensure that food is chewed well.

2/ Tying up, or azoturia, was once called Monday morning sickness, since it often affected work animals following rest during the weekend. As with colic, changes in routine feeding and exercise can contribute to a horse tying up, and some horses seem predisposed to the problem. An inconsistent or sporadic riding schedule or demanding more work than a horse is fit to perform, particularly when a horse is well-fed and stalled, sometimes makes tying up more likely. Although research is incomplete, hormonal imbalances, electrolyte levels, vitamin E and selenium deficiencies, and other factors are also thought to contribute to the problem.

Tying up causes the muscles, usually in the hindquarters, to become rigid and stiff or even to spasm, and a horse often refuses to move. He may stretch out as he stands, as if trying to relive stomach pain, somewhat like a colicked horse might. The colicked horse often tries to roll, but the tied-up horse seldom moves willingly.

When a horse ties up, the muscles are damaged and a byproduct is created that becomes apparent when the horse's urine darkens in color, and that sometimes damages the kidneys as well.

Treatment varies, but the first step is not to move the horse until the veterinarian arrives. He might administer pain medication, electrolytes or intravenous fluids, and antibiotics, depending on how severely a horse ties up. Management practices that may help minimize the problem include feeding an adequate, but not grain-rich diet, reducing grain on days when the horse is not ridden, and maintaining a regular exercise routine.

3/ Founder, or laminitis, can occur when a horse has been allowed to graze lush pasture, has consumed large quantities of cold water when he's overheated, has been ridden excessively on hard surfaces, has consumed a large quantity of grain, or as a secondary complication from other health problems. Founder affects a horse's feet—more often the front feet—and the sensitive laminae in the hoof becomes inflamed, and in some cases, the horse's coffin bone rotates down, toward the sole. When that happens, a horse can become crippled and may need to be destroyed if the damage is great.

A foundered horse often stands with his weight shifted to the rear, in an effort to relieve pain in the front feet, which normally bear the most weight. In severe cases, a horse often lies down because he is too uncomfortable to stand. The inflammation may cause heat in the hoof, and the sole may become tender. Treatments vary, but it's crucial to consult your veterinarian immediately if you suspect founder. The quicker the treatment, the less likely that a horse will become permanently crippled.

4/ Heat stroke can occur in horses, just as with people. Because of a horse's body mass, it's sometimes difficult for him to get rid of excess body heat, especially when the air is hot or the humidity is high enough to slow evaporation. Excessive exercise under extreme conditions often results in heat stroke.

As a result, a horse can become lethargic, lose his appetite, refuse commands, experience convulsions, or even die. It's important to lower the horse's body temperature as soon as possible. Hose his legs or along the neck, where the flow of blood is near the skin surface, to help cool his core temperature, keep him in the shade, and use fans to circulate cooler air over his body to bring relief until the veterinarian can arrive.

## First-Aid Kit

Cuts and scrapes are treated on horses in much the same way they are treated in humans. Shallow, superficial wounds can be flushed with an antiseptic solution, then treated with an all-purpose ointment. Maintain a close watch for possible infection in any wound, and be sure your horse has had a tetanus vaccination.

It's up to you to determine if a wound is severe enough to warrant a veterinarian's attention. In case of a severe wound, a pressure bandage can be applied to control bleeding until he arrives. For puncture wounds, it's important to ensure that the foreign object is no longer imbedded in the horse's flesh or hoof.

The veterinarian can clean a severe wound, using a local anesthetic if necessary, probe it for foreign matter, sew it closed if that's required, administer anti-inflammatory or antibiotic medications, as well as pain-relieving ones, or even X-ray an injury. But you must provide the recommended follow-up treatment at home to ensure your horse's good health.

It's a good idea to keep a few items on hand for emergency medical treatment, both in your barn and your trailer. Equine illness and injury are not confined to home. A small tool box or fishing tackle box is good for storing the supplies. Small items can go in the tray compartments, and larger ones below. Over time, you will probably add to your medical supplies, but here's a list of basic items to have on hand.

1/ Thermometer. If you know its proper use and what your horse's normal temperature is, the information is valuable to a veterinarian helping you treat a sick horse.

2/ Stethoscope. Like the thermometer, a stethoscope is of no benefit unless you know what constitutes a normal pulse rate or normal gut sounds for your horse. Again, this knowledge can be important in describing an illness to a veterinarian.

3/ Alcohol. You'll need it for disinfecting or for cleaning a thermometer.

4/ All-purpose antiseptic ointment. This should suffice for any minor cuts and scrapes.

5/ Antiseptic cleansing solution. This is used to flush out wounds.

6/ Electrolytes. These are good to have on hand during extremely hot weather or if you suspect dehydration.

7/ Bandaging materials. Keep a few non-stick wound pads on hand, along with a wide roll of gauze. Adhesive tape and scissors are a necessity, too.

8/ Vetrap™ or elastic bandage. Having either of these on hand makes it easier to protect equine wounds in awkward places. The Vetrap sticks to itself, and the elastic bandages will stretch to conform to a horse's anatomy. Be cautious in wrapping a wound, taking care not to get the bandage too tight.

9/ Pressure bandages. Disposable diapers work well as a pressure bandage, or a leg quilt will suffice as well.

10/ Hoof pick. When you suspect lameness, always pick the feet clean first, to ensure that something has not become imbedded in the hoof.

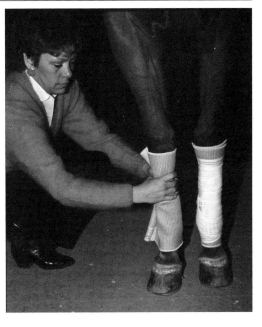

*If necessary, have a veterinarian show you how to wrap a leg, so you'll know how, should the need arise.*

11/ Slip-on boot or duct tape. A slip-on boot is convenient to protect an injured hoof. If necessary, you can cover the hoof with gauze or a diaper, then wrap it with duct tape for a short-term, protective covering.

12/ Fencing pliers. If you need to pull a horseshoe for emergency treatment, or tighten one to prevent problems, you can get the job done with fencing pliers, in an emergency. Fencing pliers are a real asset if a horse becomes tangled in wire.

13/ Medications. Pain-relieving medications, for example, or anti-inflammatories are good to have on hand, again, providing you know how to administer them. Ask your veterinarian for assistance and understand that many medications can be administered only with his supervision.

14/ Health-care book. Keep a good health-care reference on hand, or make your own, adding information as you learn health-care procedures.

One word of caution: It's best to avoid old-time remedies that well-meaning friends might offer when your horse is sick or injured. While an occasional old-time treatment might help, most of them cause more harm than good. Always consult an equine veterinarian.

# HOOF CARE

## 20

MOST people are familiar with the old saying, "no foot, no horse." There's a reason for that—it's true. Your first horse is no better than the four feet on which he stands. It's to your benefit to learn about hoof care.

As the horse developed during centuries past, nature provided for his hoof care, with natural wear trimming the hoofs as he roamed. Following the principle of nat-

ural selection, the hardiest horses, who could best escape predators, survived—in other words, the horses with good feet and legs. Today, horses must depend on mankind for adequate hoof care.

Although it isn't necessary for you to become a master farrier, or horseshoer, you should be familiar with some aspects of hoof care. This includes understanding how the parts of a hoof function, the

*Providing regular hoof care is an important aspect of equine management.*

importance of cleaning a horse's feet regularly, and the need for trimming or shoeing a horse. The better your knowledge, the better you will be able to communicate with a veterinarian or farrier, should your horse have a hoof problem.

## Parts of the Hoof

The hoof is a complex, weight-bearing structure that helps absorb shock and aids in blood circulation. Knowing a little about the structure will aid you in maintaining a healthy hoof.

1/ Hoof wall. This bears a horse's weight. Horsemen often speak of the hoof wall, the horny outer protective covering, by describing a particular portion of it. The toe, of course, is at the front of the hoof. The quarter is along either side of the hoof, between the toe and the heel, which is at the rear of the foot. Quarter cracks, or sand cracks, sometimes occur in a hoof wall that is extremely dry.

2/ White line. This is where the hoof wall and sole join. The white line should be uniform in appearance and color. Black areas or irregular thickness in the white line can be indicative of potential problems.

3/ Sole. The larger, light area on the bottom of the hoof is the sole. Its texture is somewhat similar to a fingernail's. Dark spots can indicate bruising or a possible puncture wound.

4/ Bars. These buttress the inner structures of the hoof. A cleft or indention is created on either side of the frog, where it joins the bars. Pay particular attention to cleaning the clefts well; they can be a breeding ground for thrush, especially in wet climates or dirty stalls.

5/ Frog. When viewed from the bottom, the frog in a horse's hoof is the triangular-shaped portion that runs, roughly, from the center of the hoof to the heel. The frog should be pliable and resilient. A strong, bad odor in the frog can indicate an infection, such as thrush, which is caused most often by excessive filth and moisture in the frog area.

## Daily Hoof Care

The best preventive measure to ensure a healthy hoof is cleaning each foot daily with a hoof pick. Use the proper procedure for picking up a horse's foot, as described earlier in the grooming chapter. Follow a

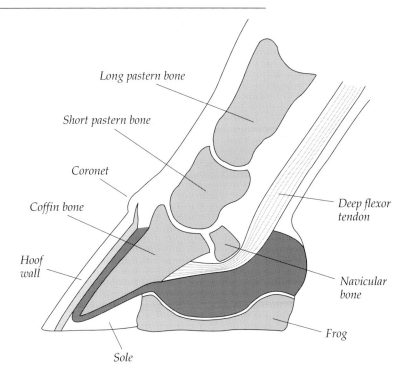

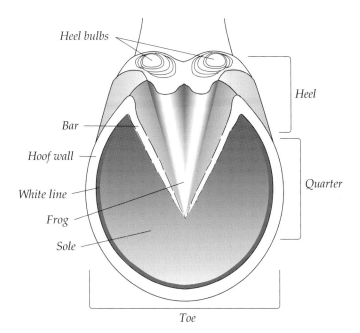

standard routine when cleaning hoofs, working from the near front foot to the near hind, the off hind, and finally the off front foot. By making hoof cleaning a part of your grooming ritual, you and your first horse can quickly become accustomed to and comfortable with the procedure.

Also use the right tool for the work. Hoof picks are inexpensive and can be purchased with an attached brush or in a folding version. Beware of cleaning a hoof with a pocketknife, especially if the blade won't

171

*When you clean your horse's feet, check for thrush and to ensure that nothing is embedded in the sole of the hoof.*

*A farrier uses a hoof knife to pare the sole when he's trimming or shoeing a horse.*

lock into place. You might cut yourself.

Clean the hoof by working from the heel toward the toe, paying particular attention to the clefts on either side of the frog. These areas are a breeding ground for thrush, which usually can be avoided with routine cleaning. As you clean, check the hoof for any bruises, puncture wounds, or embedded objects.

This is also a good time to check the hoofs for moisture content. Dryness is a common problem, especially for stalled horses or those confined to dry lots, and can cause splits in the hoof walls, a loss of elasticity in the frog, and contracted heels. Moisture evaporates from a horse's hoof and must constantly be replaced to maintain a quality hoof.

Water is a natural hoof conditioner, so it's not necessarily unhealthy for a horse occasionally to stand in muddy areas of the pasture. In fact, some horsemen intentionally overfill pasture water troughs so that horses must stand in the moisture each time they drink. But be aware that too much moisture can soften feet excessively. Also, split and cracked hoofs can result from frequently changing ground conditions—from too wet to too dry.

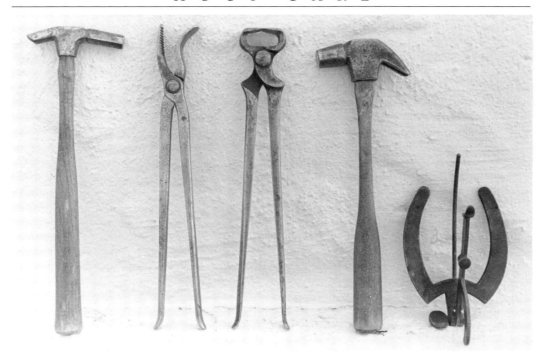

In addition to the hammers, as shown, a farrier often uses clinchers (second from left) to bend the end of the nail, once it has been cut or twisted off. Nippers (center) are used much like toenail clippers, to trim an extremely long hoof. The gauge (at right) is used to check the angle of the hoof.

There are also many commercial hoof dressings on the market today. Whatever hoof conditioner you select, remember that regular use is required by most in order to promote a healthier hoof.

# Trimming and Shoeing

A horse's hoof can grow up to about ½ inch a month, with more growth, sometimes, in the spring. Hoofs should be trimmed on a regular basis, about every 4 to 6 weeks, to help ensure the proper angle of the hoof and that a horse's weight is distributed as evenly as possible over the hoof in a balanced manner. A trim also helps level uneven hoof growth. Too extreme a hoof trim places undue stress on a horse's lower leg or foot, and often a horse trimmed too short moves "ouchy."

The tools a farrier uses in trimming a hoof are a hoof knife, nippers, and a rasp. Once the hoof has been cleaned with a hoof pick, a farrier uses the knife to pare dead sole away from the foot and to

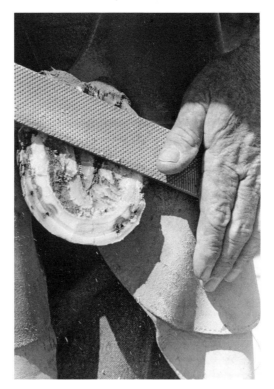

Rasping a horse's hoof is often compared to filing our fingernails.

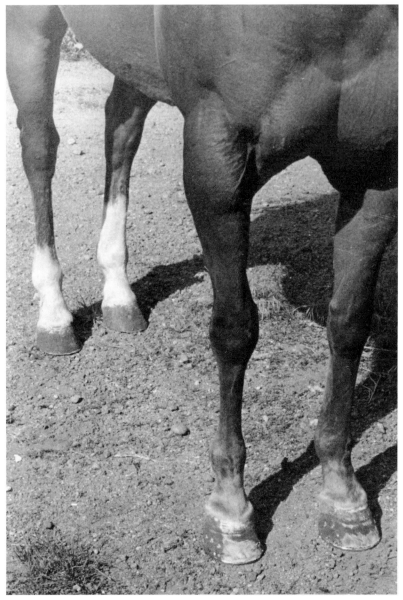

*When shod, a horse's feet should be fairly uniform in appearance, with the angle of slope on both front feet about the same, just as it should be similar on the hind pair of feet.*

remove ragged pieces of the frog, which is naturally shed periodically. If necessary on an extremely long foot that shows much growth, the farrier uses nippers to remove the excess, prior to rasping the foot. Rasping creates a level surface to bear a horse's weight.

Shoeing is necessary to protect the hoofs of horses ridden on rocky terrain or may sometimes be necessary to correct abnormal conditions in a hoof. As with trimming, horses must be reshod every 4 to 6 weeks. The shoes, however, can be reset or used more than one time. How many times depends on the amount of wear.

In addition to a hoof knife, nippers, and rasp, when shoeing, a farrier often uses a hoof gauge to check the angle of the hoof and its length. This ensures that both front and rear pairs of feet are evenly balanced. Once the shoe has been shaped to fit the horse, it is nailed on with a shoeing hammer, which can then be used to twist off excess length in the nail. A properly inserted nail does not hurt a horse, and the head of the nail should fit snugly in the shoe. Once the end of the nail has been cut or twisted off, the nail is clinched tight against the hoof wall, either with tongs or a block and hammer.

A variety of preformed horseshoes are on the market and require only minimal shaping before being nailed on the horse. These are sometimes referred to as ready-made or keg shoes, or cold shoes, and will suffice for most normal shoeing situations. Cold shoes don't require heating in order to be shaped to fit the hoof. Handmade or custom shoes, however, are made from a straight bar of stock that has been heated in a forge and then shaped to fit the hoof. Specialty shoes, such as sliding plates for reining horses, are usually handmade. Needless to say, handforged shoes are more expensive.

Many specialty shoes are available to help improve the action of a horse's foot when it's in flight. Half-rounds or rocker-toed shoes, for example, can improve the breakover in a horse's foot action, or weighted shoes may be used to alter the foot's flight pattern. Therapeutic shoes, such as an egg-bar or a heart-bar, are commonly prescribed to correct foot problems, as are pads, which can be inserted under a shoe to help protect the sole of a horse's hoof. Other shoes can help provide traction and feature screw-in studs for use in snow or ice.

If your veterinarian or farrier recommends you use a special shoe of some sort, be sure you understand why the use of that shoe is suggested. Also be sure that you are taking all the necessary measures in your daily management to minimize any hoof problem.

Establishing a good relationship with a farrier is as important as maintaining a good one with your veterinarian. Selecting a farrier isn't always easy, and horsemen in sparsely populated areas sometimes have little choice. Again, rely on the help of good horsemen in your area to find a reliable farrier, or ask your veterinarian if there is one he works with on a regular basis. Try your best to have a cooperative relationship between you, your veterinarian, and your farrier.

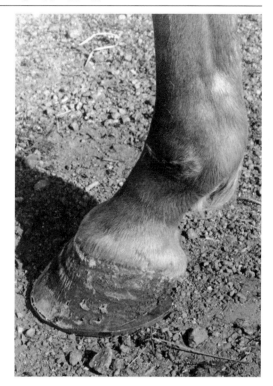

*This shoe has been extended beyond the hoof wall in a corrective process, to encourage the contracted heels to spread outward in their growth. The hoof is also dry and brittle and would probably benefit from the application of hoof dressing.*

175

The *Western Horseman*, established in 1936, is the world's leading horse publication.
For subscription information: 800-877-5278. To order other *Western Horseman* books: 800-874-6774.
*Western Horseman*, Box 7980, Colorado Springs, CO 80933-7980.

# Books Published by Western Horseman Inc.

**BACON & BEANS** by Stella Hughes
144 pages and 200-plus recipes for popular western chow.

**BARREL RACING** by Sharon Camarillo
144 pages and 200 photographs. Tells how to train and compete successfully.

**CALF ROPING** by Roy Cooper
144 pages and 280 photographs covering the how-to of roping and tying.

**CUTTING** by Leon Harrel
144 pages and 200 photographs. Complete how-to guide on this popular sport.

**FIRST HORSE** by Fran Devereux Smith
176 pages, 160 black-and-white photos, about 40 illustrations. Step-by-step, how-to information for the first-time horse owner and/or novice rider.

**HEALTH PROBLEMS** by Robert M. Miller, D.V.M.
144 pages on management, illness and injuries, lameness, mares and foals, and more.

**HORSEMAN'S SCRAPBOOK** by Randy Steffen
144 pages and 250 illustrations. A collection of popular handy hints.

**IMPRINT TRAINING** by Robert M. Miller, D.V.M.
144 pages and 250 photographs. Learn how to "program" newborn foals.

**LEGENDS** by Diane C. Simmons
168 pages and 214 photographs. Includes these outstanding early-day Quarter Horse stallions and mares: Barbra B, Bert, Chicaro Bill, Cowboy P-12, Depth Charge (TB), Doc Bar, Go Man Go, Hard Twist, Hollywood Gold, Joe Hancock, Joe Reed P-3, Joe Reed II, King P-234, King Fritz, Leo, Peppy, Plaudit, Poco Bueno, Poco Tivio, Queenie, Quick M Silver, Shue Fly, Star Duster, Three Bars (TB), Top Deck (TB), and Wimpy P-1.

**LEGENDS 2** by Jim Goodhue, Frank Holmes, Phil Livingston, Diane C. Simmons
192 pages and 224 photographs. Includes these outstanding Quarter Horses: Clabber, Driftwood, Easy Jet, Grey Badger II, Jessie James, Jet Deck, Joe Bailey P-4 (Gonzales), Joe Bailey (Weatherford), King's Pistol, Lena's Bar, Lightning Bar, Lucky Blanton, Midnight, Midnight Jr, Moon Deck, My Texas Dandy, Oklahoma Star, Oklahoma Star Jr., Peter McCue, Rocket Bar (TB), Skipper W, Sugar Bars, and Traveler.

**LEGENDS 3** by Jim Goodhue, Frank Holmes, Diane Ciarloni, Kim Guenther, Larry Thornton, Betsy Lynch
208 pages and 196 photographs. Includes these outstanding Quarter Horses: Flying Bob, Hollywood Jac 86, Jackstraw (TB), Maddon's Bright Eyes, Mr Gun Smoke, Old Sorrel, Piggin String (TB), Poco Lena, Poco Pine, Poco Dell, Question Mark, Quo Vadis, Royal King, Showdown, Steel Dust, and Two Eyed Jack.

**NATURAL HORSE-MAN-SHIP** by Pat Parelli
224 pages and 275 photographs. Parelli's six keys to a natural horse-human relationship.

**REINING, *Completely Revised*** by Al Dunning
216 pages and over 300 photographs showing how to train horses for this popular event.

**ROOFS AND RAILS** by Gavin Ehringer
144 pages, 128 black-and-white photographs plus drawings, charts, and floor plans. How to plan and build your ideal horse facility.

**STARTING COLTS** by Mike Kevil
168 pages and 400 photographs. Step-by-step process in starting colts.

**THE HANK WIESCAMP STORY** by Frank Holmes
208 pages and over 260 photographs. The biography of the legendary breeder of Quarter Horses, Appaloosas, and Paints.

**TEAM PENNING** by Phil Livingston
144 pages and 200 photographs. Tells how to compete in this popular family sport.

**TEAM ROPING** by Leo Camarillo
144 pages and 200 photographs covering every aspect of heading and heeling.

**WELL-SHOD** by Don Baskins
160 pages, 300 black-and-white photos and illustrations. A horseshoeing guide for owners and farriers. The easy-to-read text, illustrations, and photos show step-by-step how to trim and shoe a horse for a variety of uses. Special attention is paid to corrective shoeing techniques for horses with various foot and leg problems.

**WESTERN HORSEMANSHIP** by Richard Shrake
144 pages and 150 photographs. Complete guide to riding western horses.

**WESTERN TRAINING** by Jack Brainard
With Peter Phinny. 136 pages. Stresses the foundation for western training.